1

Library of Congress Cataloging-In-Publication Data

The Dead Christian
"Where is the Heart Beat of God?"

This book is dedicated to TEAM DREAM and the TWC Connectors
Your continued service is making a difference in humanity!

I believe so much in the message of this book. I want to connect with you and thank you personally for picking up this excellent read. If you are on social media please take a creative photo of you and "The Dead Christian" or the book alone and connect with me (tag me) on Facebook™ Periscope™ or Instagram™ @WendelDandridge

Thank you for helping me
"Connect People Back to God and Humanity"
Dare to Dream
Wendel Dandridge

COOLING BOARD OF CONTENTS

The Death of Christianity

If you aren't in the medical field you probably are unaware that there is certain protocol in order to pronounce someone dead. Believe it or not there are actual templates that doctors and physicians will use in order to ensure that a death pronouncement has been done properly. In my personal research I was able to discover that there are 5 specific things that need to take place for an effective declaration of death:

1. Correctly identify the patient.
2. Note that the patient is NOT hypothermic. The individual has to be warm and dead.
3. Note that there is no spontaneous movement. No verbal or tactile stimulation. No pupillary light reflex. No breathing or lung sounds. And that there is no heartbeat or pulse.
4. Communicate with the family, notify the organ donor, post mortem services, autopsy or chaplain.
5. Notify the coroner. This should be done within 24 hours with the cause of death being expresses at natural, unusual circumstances or trauma.

It is interesting to note that many of the above mentioned things we can actually parallel to the present day church. As a matter of fact I would like to, as a licensed and ordained Pastor in the Christian church, make an official proclamation of the Dead Christian. I am sure I can use the same template used by physicians:

*"I have been called to the bedside of the church to pronounce that patient Christian has died. No spontaneous movements were present. There was no response to verbal or tactile stimuli. Pupils were mid-dilated and fixed. No breath sounds were appreciated over either lung field. No carotid pulses were palpable. No heart sounds were auscultator over entire precordium. Patient pronounced dead at present day. Family and resident were notified. Chaplain and post mortem services offered. The family has declined organ donation. Patient's major medical illness was **relevancy.** Confirmed and witnessed by God's eyes"*

You are right to assume that this text will be a little hard hitting on the plight that I believe is facing the existence of Christianity. Every year there are countless people who, not only stray away from organized religion but also, lose their faith. I believe this decline in faith is not just related to faith in God but also faith in humanity. As we continue to view and face terroristic acts, poverty, genocide and health disparities, people are asking the serious questions about human agency in the world. They are asking, "Where is God?"

I am sure there are some people who will critique these words as slightly harsh towards the church. However, I believe that these words are precisely what the church universal needs to hear. Engage with me in a small synopsis and critique of the vocabulary I chose to use in the declaration of death to Christian.

1. "The bedside of the church". I believe the church has been on its sickbed for some time. It has become evident that many churches have become revolving doors for people searching for hope and action in humanity. Christianity has become a religion that has struggled to remain relevant to this millennial generation.

2. "No spontaneous movements". What major advancements have been made by Christians in the last 50 years that would warrant the title of a movement? What major historical events can be pinpointed to Christian influence? A spontaneous movement is one unexpected. What have Christians done do shake up the culture of current society?

3. "No response to verbal or tactile stimuli". How long has the church and Christians heard the cries of community to serve, but have turned a deaf ear to the true needs of humanity? There are countless causes that have called for the presence of Christians. Unfortunately their return message has been silence.

4. "Pupils were mid-dilated and fixed". It is interesting to note where the focus of many Christians and churches have gone: to self. The Christian community has become focused on self-preservation instead of preservation of The Great Commission established by Jesus.

5. "No breath sounds". Many churches and Christians have become silent to the issues that perplex the world and the communities they are located in. "No breath sounds" translates to silence. The religious community has become mute regarding issues that affect humanity.

6. "No carotid pulses". Where is the pulse of Christianity? Where is the pulse of the church? How, and why, is it that Christian service is no longer felt in our communities? A pulse is determined by what the practitioner feels on the outside of the body in order to determine the internal functions. The "feel" of Christianity can be felt from the inside of the church walls. What I seek to uncover is how the pulse is felt by those who are on the outside of the church.

7. "No heart sounds were auscultator". Where is the heartbeat of God being heard in the actions of the church and Christians? In order to confirm the pulse of the body the sound of the heart must be heard. It is possible that what is felt via the pulse isn't consistent with what is actually occurring in the body. This has become true with the church universal.

8. "Patient's major medical illness was relevancy". There was a time when Christians had an impact in the world and in humanity at large. What significant relationships are still present today? The illness of the church and Christianity is significance. If we are going to revive the faith humanity in humanity we will have to revisit the importance of Christianity in humanity.

I am beginning to notice a trend amongst people who profess to be Christians. They do nothing, or very little, that would be evidence to their profession of faith. I'm not talking about church attendance, prayer time, scripture reading, and worship participation. These are all things most Christians are good at. These faith displays are simple to execute for most people. While reluctant some weeks, it's fairly easy to find a church service to attend. Talking to God can be done at any point in the day. The bible is the best-selling book in history. However, I would like to address the heart of Christianity that I personally see taking its last breath; service to humanity.

As we look out into the world are we seeing the love of God displayed? As the need for moral consciousness rises, who is taking the lead in serving the disparities of the world? There are countless Christians, and devote religious people, who profess faith. However I am concerned with the number of those who actually act out their profession. Service to humanity, in my opinion, is the heart of Christianity. To me it is the root and pure essence of our existence. In the pages to follow we are going to discover how service is not just our Christian responsibility but also our human obligation.

That's right! I don't think the problem is church attendance or church participation for Christians. I do believe personal devotion is important in the life of a Christian. However, the heartbeat of God is slowly leaving the earth because I believe the hands and feet of God (Christians) have become lazy in the areas of community service and missions projects. Dead Christians have become silent to the social and economic injustices the still plague the globe. Media doesn't mention many of these disparities anymore, and social media has become so flooded with narcissistic posts that we have lost the consciousness that service to humanity is still necessary.

Studies have actually shown over the years the decline in Christianity and I believe lack of service is the main cause for its degeneration. **Christians have become dead to humanity.** Napp Nazworth, Christian Post Reporter, writes, "The decline in Americans who identify as Christian shown by a new Pew report is mostly due to those with weak church ties no longer identifying as Christian." (Nazworth, 2015) There was a time in culture where a person could easily identify a Christian. You would make the assumption based on what you saw being done in the environment you were observing. Interesting enough, this supposition wasn't made by their church attendance or by their personal devotion. However, in history past there was a time Christians were known by their works.

When we look at and analyze the early church, the Christian community was known for what they did and not for their worship. Keep in mind the formation of the church we are familiar with today did not take full formation until many years pasted from Jesus' death and resurrection. The congregations we have come to know today took time to develop. The liturgies and worship experiences we have today were not present in the early church. There was no praise and worship team or choir. There was no hype man or worship presider. There was no order of worship. There were no Pastors and Deacons and Elders. There were no budget meetings taking place. The above mentioned elements of church today took time to formulate. Yes, the message of Jesus' resurrection and the house meetings were a part of the Christian movement. However the birth of the church took place in the book of "Acts" for a reason. People knew that God was real and the spirit of God was present on the earth through the **works** of Christians. People weren't running to Christianity in order to get a spiritual high or to have a worship experience. People were attracted to this movement because it was centered on the altruistic acts of service and selflessness.

17

There was a point in history where if you heard of a house being built for a single mother in a low income neighborhood you would assume Christians were building it. If you saw people in the city doing a clothing drive or feeding the homeless you would assume they were Christians. If you heard of a father being reunited with his family after completing a drug program, you would assume the program was provided by the church. If there was an issue of crime in an area where a church was present, there was a time when churches would open their doors as a safe haven for people that were victimized.

Today, the problem is if there was a child walking home from school and needed a place to go to get away from the drug dealer trying to recruit them, they would be met by a locked church door or a buzzer to get in. Today, if a single mother of three kids needed help paying rent the church would make her go through a 60 day application and approval process only to be told that she can receive half the funds should she come up with the rest. Today, land has become great real estate for sanctuaries with no soup kitchens, food pantries or outreach services. To the same degree, there are countless organizations and communities crying out for the help of True Christians, but Dead Christians have become too busy to serve or make themselves available for anything outside of their church sponsored events.

I think it is a horrible misrepresentation of Christ's message for Christians to be absent in the community.

Another interesting dynamic about Christianity is the number of people who have completely disassociated from the label of "Christian" all together. Sarah Pulliam Bailey of the Washington Post writes, "Christianity is on the decline in America, not just among younger generations or in certain regions of the country but across race, gender, education and geographic barriers. The percentage of adults who describe themselves as Christians dropped by nearly eight percentage points in just seven years to about 71 percent, according to a survey conducted by the Pew Research Center. (Baily, 2015) At one point in history people were excited to be a part of this community of believers and service minded individuals. There was a moment in time where having a 'spiritual walk/connection' was just as important to someone as their education, health and career. Now when we look out into the world people have the impression that they can do with, or without, religion and spirituality.

To me, this mindset of non-spiritual necessity, is personal suicide. I live with the philosophy, like many True Christians, that *we are spirits, living in a body and possessing a soul.* Unfortunately, there are people in the world who only give attention to the body and the soul. People who tend to the needs of the body and are controlled by the desires and wishes of the soul. They spend no time, and have no concern, developing the health of their spirit. Some religions would call the spirit 'energy' or the 'God self'. My position is the world is in the condition it's in because humans are satisfied with the mortal. Humanity has become comfortable feeding the flesh. Humanity has become comfortable chasing the dreams, wishes and passions of today with no concern for their eternal footprint in time. We have become so numb to suffering, death and the disparities of humanity that we have accepted life the way it is. This is what separates Dead Christians from the early church. They were unhappy with seeing the sufferings of this world and chose to make a difference through their service.

At one point in antiquity it was cool to be a Christian. I remember the WWJD (What Would Jesus Do) trend and how people who didn't attend church were sporting this message. There was a time when people bragged about their churches and religious leaders. There was a time in history where Christians were excited about service opportunities. There was a moment when Christians were on the front line for humanitarian issues. Nonetheless what we have noticed over time is the unfortunate fact that even liars who want to feel like they belong to the "in crowd" won't describe themselves as Christians. People have become so comfortable with being of no religious affiliation at all that even the pretend Christians are disappearing.

Baily also writes, "What we're seeing now is that the share of people who say religion is important to them is declining." (Baily, 2015) I believe the primary reason for this shift of religious importance is directly connected to the Christian's involvement with humanity. A thing will never be important to an individual if it has no value or significance to the individual. Again, I believe the Christian has died from a server case of non-relevancy. Years ago I came to the realization as to why people 'join' churches. Some of the benefits to joining a community of believers are self-serving within themselves. A member receives free counseling from their Pastor. In the event you chose to get married, you can get free wedding services from your Pastor. The ultimate perk to church membership is that when you die you won't have to pay to rent the church out for your service or feed your family after your memorial.

Please don't misinterpret my statement to say that all people join churches for selfish reasons. But when was the last time you heard of a ministry that prided themselves for bringing people back to God for the purpose of service?

Clyde Kilough writes for lifehopeandtruth.com. He published a very interesting page answering the question, "Why is Christianity becoming irrelevant?". One of the major points he makes in his writing is how Christianity today looks nothing like what, I believe, Jesus intended for it to look like. I have always pondered the question in my own ministry that, "if Jesus were alive today would He recognize the Christian movement that was started over 2000 years ago?" Would He see us serving, caring, loving and giving? Or would Jesus be unable to recognize the movement because it has been enclosed by largely erected sanctuaries used solely for the purpose of worship and not for outreach? In my opinion the church universal resembles very few characteristics made evident in the early writings of those who pilgrimed the faith.

If the first Christians stood face-to-face with present day Christians what would that faceoff look like?

Clyde writes, "We've been doing the same ever since. Christianity came on the scene; but from its inception, people quickly started altering nearly everything about it. For humans to try to "improve" on God is not only arrogant and presumptuous, it also renders our religions irrelevant. The legitimacy of Christianity is totally dependent on whether its creator-Jesus the Christ, who was God on earth-is involved and active in it. If He isn't, its irrelevant." (Kilough, 2015) I agree with his observation. We have done a great job pushing for the advancement and improvement of the worship experience for people. But what have Christians done to make it easier for people to connect and serve the needs of humanity. There are countless things the church has done in order to make coming together convenient and exciting. What tends to perplex the millennial Christian is how hard it's become to get involved and serve. What perplexes the millennial worshipper is the scarcity of opportunities to be of service. The Worship Center has experienced exponential growth because of the people who come to us and say, 'my old church made it too difficult to get involved' or 'my old church wasn't doing half the projects you all are involved in'.

The truth of the matter is what started as a movement and a model for service to humanity has become a self-serving machine for religious preservation.

Clyde simplifies his statement by saying, "if Christianity isn't changing people, it isn't relevant." (Kilough, 2015) I would like to add to his statement that if Christianity isn't birthing change agents it will become irrelevant.

I still find it amazing at the masses of people who attend church on Sunday morning for hours at a time, but leave with no sense of moral responsibility to change the communities in which they live, learn and lead. It is a sad state of affair at the number of people who claim to be Christian but never experience the transfer of grace that God has made available to them. I am sure it breaks the heart of God to see people refuse to identify themselves as Christ followers when they are involved in community projects. It must be noted the increased level of corporate involvement in our communities because church involvement is at an all-time low. No longer do we see church vans unloading in opportunity areas. What we now see are t-shirts marked with corporate logos taking the place of the church.

What consistent action does your church have in the community? But more importantly, what are you, if you identify as Christian, doing consistently to make your mark on the moral compass of humanity?

Ed Stetzer of *Christianity Today* keeps it simplistic by giving us three reasons Christians are not involved in the church or community: (Stetzer, 2014)

1. *"Some people feel useless."* These individuals feel as if they do not have anything significant to offer in ministry. One interesting dynamic of the church is that many Christians feel as though they have nothing to bring to the table because everything is already being done. It would be thought-provoking to question how many Christians desire service opportunities but find it difficult to plug in without attending a meeting, a class or a prerequisite to serve?

2. *"Some people are hurting."* The truth is Christians have been hurt by other Christians and churches. Because of their past, Christians have become hesitant about getting involved again. The heartbeat of God has stopped beating because each day a member of the body at large is being damaged by other members. How can a Christian be expected to serve when those they are serving with don't show the individual how valued they are to the whole? Hurt people hurt other people. However, at some point there has to be the conscious decision to heal the body as a whole.

3. **"Some people are lazy."** Let's just be honest. Christianity is, in my personal opinion, the easiest religion to claim and be a part of. Let's also be honest with the fact that some people just don't want to serve. Some Christians would rather be objects of the faith and not partners in the movement of ethical service. Christianity is, in my view, one of the only religions you can profess with no necessary display of devotion.

There are various types of Christians that populate the world: The weak Christian, The non-relevant Christian, The Dead Christian. What they ultimately equate to is the silent heartbeat of God on earth. The truth is the Christian faith is on the decay. People have stopped believing in the message of Christ because people have stopped seeing the work of Christ being manifested in the world. Christians have become a passive community that would rather respond to a call of action instead of being the leaders who call for change. Dead Christians would prefer to wait until they are needed, instead of finding those communities that need them most. Dead Christians will wait until a situation has gone from bad to worse before they give any attention to it. Dead Christians will delay until it is a fad to serve. Dead Christians will wait until the commercials air before they chose to become involved.

The relevancy of Christianity has been trumped by the irrelevancy of Christian's desire to aid in the inequalities present in society. Christian's unwillingness to serve, in my opinion, functions as a silencer to Christ's message. If faith is on the decline so is the wellbeing of humanity. If moral change agents remain silent to the issues of the marginalized, hope for humanity is dismal. On the other hand there is hope for this faith; but it can only come when Christians become conscious of their assignment to be the hands, feet and heartbeat of God here on earth.

THE ISSUES

If Christians Weren't Dead why are Humanitarian Issues still Alive?

There is proof to suggest Christians have croaked. Outside of what was mentioned in the previous chapter, there are other proofs to suggest the presence of Christians in the scope of humanity is waning. One could attempt to prove the opposite, however the below mentioned items are on the rise; suggesting the presence of help and hope is dwindling.

My opinion is if True Christians were out doing the work of Christ we would see a drop in the issues that infect civilization. Instead, what we notice in the scope of society is the commonness of social issues. What can be observed is the largely growing population of the marginalized. What we see happening in the world is a large divide between the church and the community; religion and humanity; salvation and society. There are some cultures who believe in the pairing of opposites. Some may be familiar with the Ying-and Yang of life. If we were to used this same conception with Christianity and humanity, when one sees a global disparity one should also see a True Christian. In the same way opposites attract, Christians should be drawn to the humanitarian issues of the world.

With the availability of resources, technology, and travel there is no excuse for why current social, economic and global issues are still as prevalent as they are. It is interesting to isolate that the below mentioned issues all have simple solutions; if Christians chose to be a part of the solution, their involvement could eradicate much of these, still widespread, problems. Many Dead Christians have the perception that a person needs multiple resources, a huge budget and a huge team to make a difference in humanity. The truth is that all a person needs is the willingness to serve and give from what God has blessed them with.

I believe organized religion is to blame as well. There are two things I find problematic with the church: 1. Most people who seek to serve must be a member to participate in functions and 2. Persons are required to go through 'validation hurdles' to serve. The fact that some churches have criteria to participate in service opportunities breaks my heart as a leader. There are some organized religious communities that require members to go through orientation and new member's classes before a person can get involved. The last time I checked, when there was a need in the biblical community, people banded together in that moment and handled it. Some religious communities and leaders have made it all too hard to get involved and serve.

I would like to present to you food for thought: According to USATODAY.com, in an article written by Katherine Muniz, "20 Ways Americans are Blowing their Money", Americans who regularly buy coffee throughout the week spend on average, $1,092 on coffee annually. Yet it costs less than this dollar amount to provide purification straws to a village in South America who still does not have the technology for clean water (54 people). Where are the Christians who drink coffee?

It should pain a Christian's heart to see these issues still exist in the world. At the same time, it should disgust all human beings to look in the mirror and call themselves 'person' and do nothing about changing these statistics. Numbers don't lie. Research is designed to shed light on ambiguous assumptions. The issues listed below should not only be statistics and data, nonetheless it should prick our hearts and make us uncomfortable.

Homelessness is a social and economic issue that is very near and dear to my heart. Why? Because in 2006 I received an eviction notice on my apartment door. I had no money to pay the past month's rent. I had no other option but to begin living out of the rear of my 1998 Chevy Blazer.

I conducted a research assignment while I was getting my master of divinity degree at the Interdenominational Theological Seminary. In this assignment I revisited this demographic of people of whom I was once a part of. My discoveries were astonishing! The homeless population in Atlanta is growing. The number of people, nationwide, that are finding it hard to keep a roof over their heads is expending. It already pains my heart that our government's only attempt to address the issue is to disburse the population. However, it is even more painful at the number of Christians and churches that have turned a blind eye to this group. With the exception of Thanksgiving and Christmas, the homeless populations around the nation go unnoticed for a large majority of the year.

There is a very subtle dynamic as to how people, including Christians, view individuals that are experiencing homelessness. We are aware when they approach our car windows. We are aware when we read the, sometimes humorous, signs held at the intersection. We are aware they sleep under bridges and in business corridors. We are aware they sleep on the front steps of churches. We are aware that there are women and children on the streets of our cities. We are aware of "Tent Cities" around our neighborhoods and urban areas. We are aware that abandoned buildings aren't really abandoned. However, many of us chose to make the person on the opposite side of our visibility as invisible.

We drive by the homeless on our way to work and school. Although we consciously see them, some of us have been guilty of looking straight through them. It is a sad state of affair but many people, including Christians have made the decision to just ignore the homeless when they "see" them. There is a majority of people who are comfortable with the idea that there will always be homeless people in our cities. Many have become comfortable with the holiday giving and absence throughout the calendar year. Here in Atlanta, in the year 2016, it was projected that over 300 homeless persons would be displaced. Do you think the Dead Christians did anything about the closing of city shelters?

People experiencing homelessness are often ignored. This is a result of our ignorant assumptions made to the condition of the person as well as their intent for help. Many people automatically assume that homeless people are either: ex-convicts, mental challenged, or substance abusers. Although some of these stereotypes have proven true there are others on the streets who were, just like many of us, just one paycheck or life event away from losing housing. Another factor is that the cost of living continues to rise in various parts of the country, while wages stays the same. Housing has become so unaffordable for many people that roommate situations, even for professional adults, is on the rise.

What has the church done? What are Christians going to do in order to help with this matter? What I don't want to do is numb the efforts of those who feed the homeless, have food drives and run soup kitchens during the course of the year. But are we doing enough? Could we be doing more? And are we thinking through our efforts to help this growing population and to prevent economic disparity? These are the serious questions I believe we need to ask the person in the mirror. I also believe there needs to be dialogue and conversation initiated between faith leaders, political influencers and the homeless population.

I have to note that "homeless" people NEED homes and not just food. Otherwise we should label them as "hungry" people.

I believe there needs to be a call to action in order to address the underline issue: the lack of housing. There has to be a strategic approach to how we combat this very serious topic. This may sound cruel, but I often laugh at churches and ministries who give food baskets to the homeless population. It's not the basket that is humorous to me, but rather the contents of the package.

Why would you give a homeless person a raw turkey or canned goods when they don't have a stove to prepare them?

To me this makes absolutely no sense. Again, the matter of homelessness is the absence of affordable housing. The question to our religious and political leaders is "how can we begin to remedy this problem?" The True Christian's approach to social issues should address the core of what's being presented. Dead Christians have bandaged diseases and diagnosed wounds. We have to get it together before the world dies on us.

The response is simple. Find affordable housing solutions. I think most Christians believe it is a huge undertaking to provide a homeless person with a home. The truth is that our idea of a home, 3 bedrooms, two bathrooms, a kitchen and a driveway, has clouded our understanding of basic necessities. People need four walls, a roof and basic utilities.

What if we simplified our efforts and provided simple and affordable housing for people living below the poverty line? For those of us who went to college, and lived in dorms, we should know firsthand that a room with a window is more than enough to get through life.

While the homeless population in on the rise in some areas of the country it is not unfathomable for Christians to come together in order to provide inexpensive and modest housing to this demographic.

It is not my intent to get rid of effective feeding programs. Nevertheless we cannot turn a blind eye to the root issue of HOMElessness. With the quantity of abandoned buildings and vacant government owned real estate, there is no excuse to the numbers of people who still have no place to lay their head.

You may not consider it a serious problem in our culture because of the two people you see panhandling on your way to and from work. On the other hand, please allow me to shed some light on your perception. "On a single day in January 2014, 578,424 people were experiencing homelessness-meaning they were sleeping outside or in an emergency shelter or transitional housing program." (National Alliance to End Homelessness, 2015) Please keep in mind this does not include the number of people that sleep on couches until they get off their feet or those who have found refuge in abandoned buildings. These numbers should be mindboggling! Other statistics have suggested that there are well over 1,000,000 Americans do not have a place to call their own.

I am sure some people would read the number 578,424 and would turn a deaf ear to the situation by stating this statistic is not so bad when there are approximately 320 million people living in the United States. As a Christian, I believe 1 person sleeping on the streets is more than enough to call for action. Christ consciousness doesn't take numbers into consideration. Christ consciousness is concerned with the individual lives that need to be touch. It is a message that provides unique hope and the expectancy of specific grace.

Although the homeless population makes up less than one percent of the national population we have been called to serve the "invisible people". Maybe this perception is why we have seen outreach to this community die. Maybe it is because people don't see it as a 'major' issue. The point of the problem is that our call to service is to help the least and the lost. If the least and the lost are present in our communities then True Christians should be active. Until the homeless population gets to 0 True Christians should be relentless in their efforts to eradicate this gap.

I also believe the reason Christians have not shown a huge interest to this community is because we have already predetermined the face of this population. When The Worship Center started feeding the homeless population of Atlanta in 2012 I was shocked and heartbroken at the number of children who would frequent our line on the first Friday of every month. Not only did we begin serving the mouths of persons who looked like working professionals, but the number of mouths that were under the age of 12 was heart breaking. "One quarter of homeless people are children. HUD reports that on any given night, over 138,000 of the homeless in the U. S. are children under the age of 18." (Quigley, 2015) The heart of God beats for the children as well.

You will hear me say this a few times throughout the rest of this text, but *if that news didn't break your heart as a Christian you should turn in your Christian card.*

What is problematic with most people, including Christians, is that we only like to address what we see; instead of searching for the environments that need our help and support.

When an issue, or cause, is in the headlines we like to rally and support. But what about the silent assassins that are killing our community, society, humanity and the Christian population itself?

We have to do better, but we also have to seek the knowledge associated with the environment to help address the issues. I don't just blame ignorant Christians, I also blame uninformed Pastors and leaders who fail at the quest for humanitarian enlightenment. We can't blame people for not knowing when Pastors only focus self-serving agendas.

How can Christians be led into social and humanitarian change when the leaders are unaware of the problems that need to be addressed?

There are other factors that attribute to homelessness. One of which most Dead Christians chose to remain quite about. "Domestic violence is a leading cause of homelessness among women. According to the National Law Center on Homelessness and Poverty (NLCHP), more than 90 percent of homeless women are victims to sever physical or sexual abuse, and escaping that abuse is a leading cause of their homelessness." (Quigley, 2015) What we can learn from this discovery is that every social and humanitarian effort is undergirded by a moral issue. If the bible serves as a moral compass, True Christians should be able to get to the root of some of these disparities. As Christians, we should be the champions and advocates for moral change.

Sex Trafficking is another one of those 'diminutive" issues that churches and Christians are afraid to address. One of the cultural issues Christians still need to address is being comfortable with the word sex in church. This three letter word is still heard as a 'dirty' word if said in the context of the church. Heaven forbid a religious leader uses this words from religious podiums. I have come to the conclusion that Dead Christians are uncomfortable with this expression because their sex lives aren't what they desire! It becomes painful to talk about things people still can't get right in their own lives.

I heard a comedian say a few years ago that he doesn't know why the church and Christians are still so afraid of the word sex; "how do you think all these little baby Christians got here? (Steve Harvey)

Sex trafficking, pornography, sex enslavement and prostitution were other issues that became near and dear to my heart while I was pursuing my Master of Divinity degree. I was enrolled in an ethics course when the professor challenged us engage with any social-ethical dilemma of our choice. While my colleagues were researching 'safe' topics, I was searching deep into the darkness of sexual ethics. What I discovered about this moral, social and economic business was jaw dropping. Yet Christians are completely unware of what lies beyond the dark shadows of the night because they are comfortable in the light they have found.

If True Christians are going to live up to the title they possess, we are going to have to get comfortable being uncomfortable. We are going to have to be willing to engage with the forbidden. We must be willing to speak up for those who have been silenced because of their condition and not their potential. True Christians can't stay in the safe zone of service.

My personal opinion is if Christians chose to rise up and regain the heartbeat of God it is going to take us engaging with situations that are literally killing and hurting humanity as a whole.

According to CNN, "More than 3,500 sex trafficking cases were reported to the National Human Trafficking Resource Center last year alone." (Ford, 2015) A person must note that these are the *reported* cases. Government and other organizations have found it difficult to penetrate this world of "Pimps" and "Johns". This number does not included pornography slaves, and those who are sexually exploited for the gain of another. Sex trafficking is a multi-billion dollar a year industry and many influential leaders participate in this immoral act of enslavement.

This reality, however, leads to a very staggering point with regards to why this moral issue has not made it to the surface of our moral compass; money. "Some traffickers in Atlanta make more than $32,000 a week. The Study also cited research findings from 2007 that Atlanta's illegal sex industry generates $290 million a year." (Ford, 2015) Not only does sex sell…sex pays. There are many persons who are making huge profits on the backs of others; or should I say, while others lay on their backs.

Meanwhile Dead Christians launch capital campaigns for church buildings.

The rate at which this "industry" (as they have now labeled it) is growing has become sickening and alarming. Nevertheless, Christians and churches see no problem. I have to applaud one ministry partner who is leading the cause here in Atlanta; The Atlanta Dream Center, who actually ministers to all elements of sexual exploitation (not solely sex slaves). But again, if Dead Christians don't see the issue it will never be a concern.

There are so many criminally associated issues that conservative Christians chose to address without even looking in the direction of human trafficking. But did you know, "Human trafficking is the third largest international crime industry (behind legal drugs and arms trafficking). It reportedly generates a profit of $32 billion every year. Of that number, $15.5 billion is made in industrialized countries." (Do Something Organization, n.d.) If Dead Christians can stand up for drugs and gun laws why can't they move one level down in order to change laws that relate to sexual exploitation? More laws need to be put in place that would advocate for women being caught in sex crimes to be treated as victims and not criminals.

Lack of Clean Water across the globe is another issue I believe Dead Christians need to turn their attention to. "More than 840,000 people die each year from a water related disease." (Water.org, n.d.) While some country populations get excited about the newest smart phone or the next luxury automobile, there are still developing countries who lack basic necessities.

Before you begin reading this section I think you should go and get yourself a glass of water.

As a matter of fact, I can probably make a safe assumption that you have bottled water somewhere nearby. Pour it in a glass if you will. But before you place your lips to this refreshing goblet of hydration I want you to consider adding a few things to your glass. Let's start with a few drops of your partner's bath water from last night. Then we can add a few drops of motor oil from your neighbor's motorcycle outside. But let's also take a ride up the road and see if we can capture some cow urine to give it a bit of flavor. As unappetizing as these ingredients my sound there are millions of people in the world who drink waters with these impurities in it. They drink the same water others bathe in. They consume the same water people wash their automobiles in. They ingest the same water that catches animal waste.

I am apologize if my sarcasm made your stomach turn, but have you come to realize there are literally hundreds of millions of people that still do not have access to the simplicity of clean water? For many of us, we have become so comfortable with our life styles to take something so simple for granted. Many of us don't just have access to clean water that dispenses from our faucet, we have the options of bottled water and even flavored water. Yet there are hundreds of children dying of dehydration and other water borne illnesses daily.

To me it is fascinating how Dead Christians can be so concerned, and will cast judgement, about drinking alcohol, yet remain silent about the absence of clean running water in developing countries.

What pains my heart all the more, and should pain yours as well, are the simple solutions that technology has introduced in order to provide pure drinking water to these populations. There are options out there from water purification straws ($19.95), to self-managed water purification systems ($2595.00), to fully functioning water wells ($4,000.00). Nonetheless, our churches will spend ten times these amounts on vacation bible school books and curriculums. Meanwhile "Dead Christians" will also pledge 4 to 5 times these amounts to building funds and Pastor Anniversary assessments.

When will we redirect our attention to the needs of humanity instead of the wants and desires of self?

In The Worship Center's first year of being opened, and with less than 100 weekly attendees, The Worship Center was able to build two water purification systems in the Dominican Republic and Ghana. Yet there are surrounding ministries that have multi-million dollar budgets that won't plant 1% of their budget into a project like this. Have Christians, and the church, become so comfortable with our blessings that we have become blind to the opportunities to bless others? The resources Dead Christians have access to are immeasurable. Yet much of these resources stay filtered through the walls of the church and never reach the community, or the globe.

Pastors, preachers, and religious leaders will often expound from the text, John 4:14 "but whoever drink the water I give them will never thirst. Indeed, the water I give them will become in them a spring of water welling up to eternal life." (NIV) Dead Christians have become so focused on Jesus being the living water and their own "springs of eternal life" to the point where Dead Christians have become spiritually dehydrated.

We should be thirsty to serve!

You may be asking, what should "Dead Christians" be doing then? There is another simple solution and answer to this question. I have already listed three resources available in order to provide relief this global problem. There are countless, and credible, organizations that have taken the lead in battling this problematic disparity. It is our responsibility as True Christians to find them and support them.

I also encourage churches and True Christians to not just send money in order to say "I gave" or "we built". Instead, challenge yourself to actually go and serve. Make the decision to use your "vacation time" at work as "service time". A mission's trip to Ghana to build a water purification system costs less than that trip to Las Vegas you've been planning!

This is the first humanitarian issue, in this text, I believe requires Christians doing a dirty word: missions. Many Dead Christians have become so comfortable with throwing money at problems that they have lost the desire to be physically active. True Christians don't mind getting out and getting our hands dirty. It may take sacrificing your 10 day trip to Paris which would cost $3700 to go to the Dominican for $600 and stay with the locals, but the impact made will be priceless.

If we are going to be True Christians of service we must also be willing to be Christians of personal sacrifice.

The numbers are staggering. Approximately "750 million people around the world lack access to safe water; approximately one in nine people." (Water.org, n.d.) There are still innumerable villages and countries that do not have the technology and resources that many other populations have been fortunate enough to receive. The good news is that this technology to make clean water accessible to developing countries is mobile and affordable. Years ago this statistic was over 1 billion! Now, because of modern technology and sourcing we have been able to lower this sum. However, there is still much work that has to be done. The True Christians goal, as with the homeless population, is to diminish this number to 0. With the number of True Christians and True Churches in the world we can end this deadly situation regarding a simple commodity.

What is even more heartbreaking is the number of children that have been effected by this global disparity. "An estimated 801,000 children younger than 5 years of age perish from diarrhea each year, mostly in developing countries. This amounts to 11% of the 7.6 million deaths of children under the age of five and means that about 2,200 children are dying every day as a result of diarrheal diseases." (Centers for Disease Control and Prevention, 2015) To see a child drink from a contaminated stream is heart breaking. What is sadder is the fact that many of these children have no other choice but to drink from these waters to survive. Taste matters not to them. Filtration is their least concern. A thirsty child needs to drink water, contaminated or otherwise. While Dead Christians feed their children soft drinks and flavored punch, there are parents who force their children to swallow brown water at birth.

If this discovery does not break your heart, or propel you to act on this issue, you have permission to relinquish your "Christian Card".

Domestic Violence is another one of those hush hush issues many Christians fall victim to but are too afraid to address publically. There are a number of women, and men, who attend our churches on Sunday morning with an excessive amount of cosmetics on in order to cover the bruises they incurred from the night before. Domestic violence is one of those issues many people can sense when someone is going through it. Why? Because many of us can identify a person who is afraid or living in fear. I have seen, and been able to pick up first hand, the traits that would identify a person who is in an abusive relationship.

The general assumption regarding domestic violence is the young girl who fell in love with the older man who had an anger problem. The reality is the face of domestic violence has changed over the years. Now we are finding women who have been married for 20 years experiencing this dark character trait of their spouse. In the same way people change, so does the dynamics of one's relationship with that change. How people handle stress and life events can trigger certain behavioral deviations. Taking this information into consideration, no person is immune from becoming a victim or a perpetrator. The numbers for men who are experiencing an abusive relationship are also on the rise.

Domestic violence is another one of those silent "in home" issues many Christians, evidently, believe should be handled in the privacy of a person's home. In most cases it is not until the victim is permanently disabled, mutated, or killed that we see attention given to these cases. I remember hearing the story of a woman who had experienced domestic violence for years and could never find refuge in her circle of Christian friends. It was something she went through alone because of the embarrassment, and judgement, she knew she would feel if they found out. When she did find the courage to approach her Pastor about her circumstance, his response was for her to "stick it out, get counseling and pray that God would change his heart."

Today she still has fragments of the bullet her husband put in her head permanently present in her skull.

She was blessed and fortunate to survive this ordeal. But it wasn't until the sound of the gun went off that people heard her voice. There are so many people who suffer in silence at the hands of a partner they love. There are dozens who believe the vows they made trump the painful experience they are in. There are those who hope and pray for a change. There are some who refuse professional help and spiritual counsel. There are multiple individuals that are too afraid to leave, yet too in love to liberate themselves from the hands, and fist, and kicks, and blows of an aggressive loved one. As True Christians, it should sadden our hearts at the number of lives lost each year by this act of misguided anger and passion.

The current statistics are shocking. Did you know that "3 is the number of women murdered every day by a current or former male partner in the U.S. 38,028,000 is the number of women who have experienced physical intimate partner violence in their lifetimes. 18,500,000 the number of mental health care visits due to intimate partner violence every year. And 10,000,000 children are exposed to domestic violence every year." (Vagianos, 2015) These numbers are too gigantic not to go unnoticed.

Not only are women suffering from the physical abuse of domestic violence, but children are experiencing psychological scars that make them: 1. afraid of the oppressor's personality type as they get older or 2. Puts them at a greater propensity to revisit these same displays of aggression as they get older as victim or aggressor. In other words, children will fear what scared them, or they will reenact and become what frightened them. Either way we must be committed to breaking the family curse.

The argument regarding domestic violence and the Christian's role as a beacon of hope and support is we can't be afraid to initiate dialogue with victims. I believe the biggest fear in our churches is the potential of discovering who the aggressors are. This discovery won't make the faith look favorable if the aggressors turn out to be influential church leaders or respected parishioners: in most situations this is the case. As Christians, our concern, as was Jesus', is that we advocate for justice on behalf of the oppressed. We must learn to advocate for those who have lost their voice in hopeless circumstances. We must speak up for those who have been forced into silence.

What needs to first happen is the creation of safe environments where victims can come without judgement or embarrassment. Secondly, we cannot be afraid to act on behalf of the victim. If nothing else the victim needs support. Domestic violence situations have proven tricky over the years. True Christians must remain delicate to the situation and understand their role to the victim and the aggressor; both should be extended the grace and love of God. Mush of this delicacy is due to the level of manipulation, fear and commitment between the couple. These factors make the situation one that cannot be approached lightly. True Christians should be willing to approach the issue with sensitivity and prayer while partnering with professionals that can effectively guide the victim through a process of restoration. Simultaneously, the aggressor will need the support necessary to work through the unhealthy behavioral expressions.

The task with this household issue is that it is exactly that: a household issue. In order to get to the root of the problem it would take us walking through the doors of people's homes instead of peeping through their windows and listening through their walls. Did you know that "Every 9 seconds in the US, a woman is assaulted or beaten? On a typical day, there are more than 20,000 phone calls placed on domestic violence hotlines nationwide. Only 34% of people who are injured by intimate partners receive medical care for their injuries." (National Coalition Against Domestic Violence, n.d.) The Dead Christian will never hear these calls or see their bruises because of their refusal to enter the dark world of domestic violence. These victim's voices will continue to go unheard because Dead Christians would rather hear about the next church meeting.

It's a sensitive topic, but what better people to show compassion than True Christians.

The **HIV/AIDS Epidemic** is still a topic most churches and Christians refuse to take a consistent role in. It amazes me at the current level of ignorance presently displayed by people around this health issue. The fact of the matter is churches have not educated their congregations and Christians have made HIV/AIDS the present day leprosy. Because of this perpetual ignorance and stigmas associated with HIV/AIDS there are countless people literally dying in silence.

I must admit it was not until I was studying for my Master of Divinity degree that I was made aware of the truths associated with this health issue. Here I was, a religious leader for over a decade, with very little knowledge and truth about this virus. To this day I remember a plethora of information that, originally, I was ignorant to. At this moment in life I was also embarrassed at the ill-informed facts I had ingrained in my mind. For years I had listened to media and stigmas as my source of information. To my surprise, much of what I was exposed to were falsities. To think, here I was an educated, successful, Pastor and community leader who was still ignorant to HIV/AIDS. What I did realize in my moment of enlightenment was that I was only ignorant because of the fear I had within myself about this health issue.

I believe there are many other Dead Christians who don't want to address HIV/AIDS because of their personal fears. Fears that include the thoughts, "People will think I have it", "People will think I'm gay", "People will think I'm promiscuous", "What if I get tested and I do have HIV?", "Will I die in a year?", "I can't imagine taking all those pills", and the worst thought of all…

"Sin is the root cause of HIV/AIDS"

If we are going to be Christians that are alive in the world we cannot be afraid of engaging with the issues that may make us feel uncomfortable. We cannot be afraid to dialogue with the lepor as to how we can provide support, healing and restoration. We must be willing to offer the same platform of the breast cancer survivor to the person who is living with HIV/AIDS. We cannot continue to support the causes and illnesses that are trendy and ignore other illnesses that are controversial. In the same way churches and ministries have "Pink Sundays" for breast cancer, we should also have "Red Sundays" to honor the courage of those in our community, and congregations, that are living with HIV/AIDS.

It is still alarming, with media and medical advancements, the number of people infected and affected by this health issue each year. "About 50,000 people get infected with HIV each year. In 2010, there were around 47,500 new HIV infections in the United States." (Center for Disease Control and Prevention, 2015) I believe these numbers will continue to rise as long as people remain irresponsible about their personal health. HIV/AIDS is not a moral issue; as others have made it out to be. HIV/AIDS is a health issue. It does not matter how a person contracted the virus, because we have discovered HIV is not only transmitted through sexual activity. With free testing now available, there is no excuse as to why people are still transmitting this virus to others unknowingly.

Why has the church, and why have Dead Christians, not taken the lead in providing healing, hope and help to people living with HIV? The answer is simple. In the same manner as the lepor in biblical times, we have deemed those who have HIV/AIDS as unclean. The first step to restoring the person is to acknowledge their personhood and not their condition. We have also made the presupposition that people living with HIV acquired this health issue through some immoral action. This assumption is another byproduct of social ignorance.

I personally know a woman who has HIV. She did not acquire it because she was same gender loving. She did not acquire it because she was promiscuous. She did not acquire it because she shared needles as a substance abuser. She acquired it through a blood transfusion while giving birth to her son. This happened a year before laws were put in place to test blood for HIV before using it for medical purposes.

Is she immoral? Is she unclean? Does her testimony matter? Does she need support? When will Dead Christians stop looking at the issues we are called to address, and see the people we are called to love through there life challenges?

I cannot close this section without allowing the numbers to speak for me. "About 1.2 million people in the United States were living with HIV at the end of 2012, the most recent year this information was available. Of those people, about 12.8% do not know they are infected." (Center for Disease Control and Prevention, 2015) I have echoed others with the statement, "The greatest risk associated with HIV is not knowing." A person knowing their status is one of the primary ways I believe we can combat this epidemic. I believe the almost 13% that are unaware they are infected are too afraid of how Dead Christians and society will treat them once they discover their status. It is a sad state of affair but a very true statement.

Many people whom I have talked to living with HIV/AIDS have said one of their initial thoughts after being diagnosed was "how will people view me?" and "how will I be accepted by (insert community)".

Dead Christians have become so judgmental, not exclusively with HIV/AIDS but with other "morally connected" issues, that we look past the person who is desperate for compassion.

Global Illiteracy is so prevalent in our churches and Dead Christians don't even realize it. Often times I will visit churches and will see this social and academic issue being displayed right in our worship experiences. Every time I go to a church and there is some form of "community" reading I make it a point not to read. It's not because I don't want to read or because I'm being defiant. It's because I am curious as to the number of people who still struggle with reading. The first time I conducted this experiment in a church I was shocked! As I continued my unofficial studies it broke my heart.

Whether it's a scripture, hymn, vision statement or mission statement being read in church, next time you are in a worship environment see how many people in the audience have troubles reading.

Read the person's lips and you will quickly find out there are people we sit next to in church unable to read past a 5th grade reading level. "According to a study conducted in late April by the U.S. Department of Education and National Institute of Literacy, 32 million adults in the U.S. can't read. That's 14 percent of the population. 21 percent of adults in the U. S. read below a 5th grade level, and 19 percent of high school graduates can't read." (Huffington Post, 2015) These numbers should prove shocking to you; a person who is actually reading! Your ability to comprehend, understand and retain information places you in a category others struggle.

This, in my opinion, should not be viewed as some passive educational issue only to be handled by a broken educational system. To the same degree, provided this new information, it is almost impossible to trust the "household" to teach the next generation the importance of reading when the current generation of adults are illiterate. We wonder why the ignorance of humanity perpetuates? Because information is often transmitted through writing, then acquired through reading.

As a college professor I noticed this dynamic amongst my students as well. It is another issue I believe "Dead Christians" need to champion. The problem with global illiteracy is that people who struggle with reading are embarrassed, and feel less then, when Rev. Dr. Pastor Deacon Michael Knowitall B.A., MBA, J.D. discovers they can't read. There is a reason why I started dropping many of my titles and intellectual accolades. People should not feel intellectually inferior to another individual, especially a True Christian.

Because it doesn't matter how many books I've published if the audience I'm seeking to sell them to can't read them.

If the numbers I listed above don't make you angry or compassionate about global literacy you should turn in your "Christian Card". We cannot continue to preach being "students of the word" when a vast number of our congregations are illiterate. We cannot push for people to read and study the bible when a large majority are unable to get through Herman Melville's classic novel Moby Dick.

I am sure many people will blame the world's educational system. I am sure others will blame parenting. But I believe this is an area where True Christians should be stepping up to make sure those who struggle with reading can get tutoring and support. Surprisingly, this isn't a social issue that costs a lot of money, time or resources to execute. All that is needed is a book and a willingness to serve. Sadly there are many Dead Christians that bask in their intellect and obtain the mindset of, "well I have mine and you have yours to get".

Many people don't see a problem with this educational dilemma because it doesn't affect them directly. In actuality it does. "According to the Department of Justice, 'The link between academic failure and delinquency, violence, and crime is welded to reading failure.' The stats back up this claim: 85 percent of all juveniles who interface with the juvenile court system are functionally illiterate, and over 70 percent of inmates in America's prisons cannot read above a fourth grade level, according to BeginToRead.com." (Huffington Post, 2015) Are we beginning to see why this issue is important? The correlation between reading and delinquent behavior should push True Christians into action; if nothing for the purpose of making our communities safer.

Again, this is one of those issues that doesn't get much media attention or even social recognition. Yet it is an issue that effects almost every area of humanity. I would suggest those who can read to spend time teaching and exposing those who can't to literature. Imagine the feeling of opening someone's consciousness to the amazing literature and information that circulates our world!

Outlined in this chapter are just a few areas I believe are crying for the attention of human agency. There are countless organizations and non-profits that have done the leg work and laid the foundation for service. They have gathered the resources and are skilled in the fields they have been commissioned to serve. How will True Christians help eradicate these problems? Who will Christians begin to partner with in order to provide manpower and additional resources to these communities? How bad do these problems have to become before they warrant the attention of those who have been commissioned, by Jesus Himself, to carry out the solutions? I've heard elders say, "It will get worse before it gets better." I would like to re-coin it to say...

It will get worse as long as Christians don't do better!

Why Dead Christians Stopped Checking into Mortuaries (Churches)

The last thing a Dead Christian wants to do is be around other Dead Christians. For this reason many people make the conscious decision not to go to church. It's not that church environments are dead. There are great entertainment centers, we call churches, which people can go to! They have screens, lights, fog machines, young hip pastors in jeans, bright smiling greeters and (at The Worship Center FREE COFFEE)! So why are Christians still not attending church?

The truth is simple…all of the above mentioned doesn't matter the new millennial Christian.

Now don't get me wrong, the above mentioned enhancements to the contemporary worship experience are amazing. There was a moment in history when the church was dead and needed a revitalization for how we gathered for worship. To be honest, these advances have had a very positive influence on the 'worship' element of Christianity. The Dead Church heard the requests of the community and made the necessary adjustments in order to keep up with the times. However, the Christians of today are seeking more than just a Sunday morning worship experience. They are looking for a way to serve. They are looking for a way to get involved. They are looking for a way to give back. They are looking for a way to sincerely "connect back to God and humanity".

This book is not designed to help churches grow their membership. This book is not designed to help Pastors grown their ministry presence. I don't want people to feel as though I am bashing the church, or Christianity as a faith. I would understand if I was a non-religious person writing this text. But as an insider of the faith I am able to write from a very specific perspective. The purpose of this text is for all of us, who claim the Christian faith, to do a self-examination as to why we profess this faith. There are dozens of faith practices for a person to choose from. From Ancient Near Eastern, to Traditional Orthodox, African Derived and New Age, people have options. What I desire is to help those who have adopted the philosophies of this Traditional Orthodox religion to come home to the original brand, and message, of the faith.

In doing my own personal research, I was able to discover some very interesting opinions as to why Christians are no longer active in the church. Why our corporate gatherings are becoming depleted each week of attendees. Why some of our mega churches are turning into hallow arenas. The funny thing is I was once a Dead Christian too. I guess you could say I had my "Paul on the road to Damascus encounter". It was my point of personal discovery. However, instead of me going from Christian hater to Christian converter, I was a comfortable Christian who needed to be converted into an uncomfortable (active) Christian.

I have encountered both ends of the spectrum: At one point I was such a super Christian I had grown numb to the social issues outside of the church. On the other hand, there was a time when I was completely fed up with Christianity and had stop going to church for the reasons outlined in this book! You can call me crazy, but I have traveled down both roads. And I am grateful for the journey. I remember the last time I "left the church" (because there was more than one occasion where I did). The level of hurt I felt as I drove off the parking lot that final time was immeasurable. As the tears began to well in my eyes I felt as though I could also fell the heart of God breaking for his people. It wasn't related to anything done to me, but I was hurt at how church people were treating non-church people. I was hurt at how Christians would turn their noses up and not want to sit next to the homeless gentleman in service. I was hurt at the gossip associated with the young lady who was discovered to be pregnant but not married. I was hurt at how Dead Christians were hurting other Christians. I remember being in a church service and literally feeling the heart of God breaking for humanity.

That's right, even the "Super Christian" can become a "Dead Christian".

I had become comfortable with my Christianity. I could have been the poster child for the "church boy" ad. At one point I was at the church 4 days a week. I attended 3-5 services a Sunday. I was in the music ministry, the Pastor of the young adult ministry, a Youth Pastor at one point, a children's church volunteer and much more! I preached. I sung. I directed the choir. I played the keyboard. I have done it all in the church. The problem was that everything I did served the churches I was a part of. I wasn't serving humanity or the community half as much as I was serving the church. I wasn't volunteering with the local organizations and nonprofits half as much as I could have. I was engulfed in doing church work to the point where I had forgotten about my work for the kingdom. This was a problem.

However, and the end of the day I had to realize my Christianity had nothing to do with how many brownie points I got for going to church and doing church people stuff. What I did realize was my Christian existence meant nothing if I wasn't following Jesus' ultimate commandment: to love and serve others. There was a time in my Christian journey where I had a serious conviction for my laziness. Here I was teaching, preaching and singing on Sunday morning, yet you would never see my face tending to the needs of the community. But then again I would notice other Dead Christians doing the same thing! Every time the church doors were opened they were front and center. Every time there was a convention or a conference they were the first to register. Every concert or musical would be packed with people looking to hear some great singing. However, when a call was put out to these same audiences for service the attendance would become fractional.

Church has become a place where love is a personality trait and not a character trait engrained in the molecular DNA of Christianity. We know what love is. We know how love is expressed. We know who we are called to love. We know where the love of Christ is needed most. We understand the importance of Christ's love in the globe. So why don't we see love in action anymore? My hypothesis is that the heartbeat of God is faint in the workings of humanity. Dead Christians are to blame, but dead churches have birth these zombies.

If you are wondering why Christians no longer attend church I may have the answer. I believe, with the help of a few scholars and commentators, I have discovered a few very valid arguments to this topic. There may a few of the below listed opinions that you, as a Christian, dead or "alive", can relate to.

Again, the purpose of this text is informational. However I hope we can all take a moment to reflect and to ask ourselves the serious question, "why am I a Christian?". But more importantly, "What am I doing in order to help make humanity better?". Our Christian lifestyle has to be more than just about the communal worship experience. Worship, prayer and devotion should not be the only practices that feed us spiritually. I believe this desire for more in the Christian experience is what has caused many people to leave the church; and ultimately organized religion. I am of the belief people stopped asking the hard questions of the church and decided to do a little self-examination. I believe people stopped making the excuse the church. Instead the excuse becomes personal will and desire.

I think one of the primary reasons people don't attend church is because, "There is no reason to. You've made it too easy…We want something more ancient than sign on the dotted line. But if membership means an invitation to study the mystery of faith deeply, to put some skin in the game with time and talent and treasure, to enter into a process of formation over the next few months whereby we openly discuss the tenants of faith." (Unknown, 2015) I believe there should be a church overhaul as to how we acclimate people through Christianity. I believe the church has mastered bringing people "to" Christ. I believe the downfall is the church fails in the area of walking people "through" Christianity. It's simple to find a church, be moved by the worship, accept Christ, and gain membership. But what happens after this moment of emotional and spiritual response? If we chose to adopt the book of Acts model, every person who came would then be prompted to serve and connect. There are many ministries who push service and connection; however much of what is presented as opportunities are self-serving for the church.

You may be encouraged to join the choir. You could be recruited as a Children's Church volunteer. You may be asked to serve on the guest services team or to join a gender specific group. My question is how many ministries have an outline of community projects for people to Jump!n to and serve? Often time's people are prompted and cheered to join a ministry within the church. I believe the true problem falls with the fact that churches don't have much happening outside the church for people to do. Imagine the impact our churches would have if we began asking the question, "Where would you like to serve outside our church?".

My inquiry is how many Christians chose to become "followers" of Christ?

In order to be a "follower" of Christ it would mean that we are going somewhere. To follow is a verb or action word. "Christ" is the title given to Jesus because of his message of service and social justice. If we are going to be "Followers of Christ" we have to be moving in the direction of Jesus' message to serve and create social change. The church has to leave the building. Christians should be constantly responding to the message and example of Christ. I believe people are drawn to Christianity for a reason. It is our responsibility as True Christian to keep the magnetic draw strong by putting our energy out in humanity. There should be such an energy that permeates the service of Christians that it not only pushes the message of Jesus, but also prompts people to move with the message. People should see Christians making a difference and feel compelled to join the movement to end the countless global disparities that are out there.

The foundation of Christianity was based on the practice of discipleship. So why are Christians not learning to follow the root of Christ's ministry? Why has service, social justice and community involvement not been engrained in the mindset of all Christians after they walk down the aisle of the church? The fact of the matter is that Christians are tired of being lazy! True Christians should be tired of the only qualification for membership (into the faith) being tithing and church attendance.

I believe one of the primary issues is we have strayed from the essence of the faith: discipleship. Teaching others how to serve has been one of the major downfalls of the church. To the same degree, Dead Christians are only breeding other Dead Christians. In our churches, small groups and personal conversations are we teaching service? Are we creating the dialogue between seasoned Christians and new Christians as to the importance of humanitarian action? What I have noticed is that much of what is taught is a self-serving theology. Some of the only times we engage in service dialogue is during the holiday season when we are made aware of the poverties around us. The world would be a better place if we had continuous conversation about our Christian obligations.

You, should you be a person who professes the Christian faith, should be desiring more. Not from the church, but from your life. You should be challenging your churches and your Pastors to challenge you more. If we want to see the church change we have to demand it. If we want to see the church change we have to quit excepting the norm. If we want to see a change in the church we have to require more of ourselves. At The Worship Center, I believe the reason people have been joining our ministry is because I, as their Pastor, refuse to just let people except Christ and do nothing for humanity. There has to be a sense of responsibility and accountability.

Most Christians know they should be serving. Most Christians know they should be giving. Most Christians know they should be raising the moral standards of life and community. Yet many Dead Christians feel no push towards service. However, what all Christians should understand is that when we meet the divine we will have to give an account for what we did while we experienced this consciousness called life. God isn't going to exclusively ask you how many times you prayed and went to church. God will ask you how many times you visited the sick. You will be asked what you did to end the spread of HIV. You will be asked how you improved the literacy of children. God will say, "I gave you the gift of eternal life, what did you do to help others live?"

The church should be an exciting place for people to Jump!n and get involved. Do you feel as though *"Your church is depressed?"* (Unknown, 2015) This is another reason why many Dead Christians, including yourself, may not attend church. Outside of the lights and fog machines on Sunday morning, there is nothing compelling and exciting about formalized church that pushes Christians to connect with humanity. The truth is there are countless people who leave church with no sense of service. It is becoming more evident that there are countless Dead Christians who have become fed up with the emotionalism of ministry and are now seeking opportunities to serve. The Pastor may have great oratorical skills. The Children's ministry may cater to newborns and advance with service through college age. The seating in the auditorium may be comfortable. But the millennials of today want to get excited about what they are able to bring to the table. The millennials of today, as narcissistic as it may be, are eager to take a selfie of themselves giving a plate of food to a homeless person. There are tons of great churches that offer a depressing service agenda. Yet we wonder why seats in our sanctuaries are empty.

Please don't confuse entertainment with excitement?

I am a firm believer the worship experience should be more than just a Sunday morning show. Rather people should be getting excited about the Christian work and involvement that happens outside of the four walls of the sanctuary. When will Christians come to a place where we challenge ourselves to be genuinely excited about service and being a part of global change?

Maybe Dead Christians have nothing to get excited about. Maybe Christianity has become a religion that "sub-surfaces" everything else. Can you remember a time when Christians prided themselves as being the best in social, community and humanitarian efforts? Do you recall a time in history where the church and Christian model was the go-to example for how moral obligation was executed in the world? Now "You do nothing well. We live in a time where excellence is highly desired." (Unknown, 2015) Many Christians and churches can't take pride for anything! It is disheartening the few that are carrying the message of service and moral obligation are doing it in their own name and not the name of Christ. Churches have ministry after ministry for every cause known to man. Yet, very little of what they do is at a level where it makes an impactful difference.

Can we, for the sake of conversation, admit that true excellence is far from the mindset of Dead Christians? That the quest to be the best at anything is far outside of our mental reach. To the same capacity, our desire to be the moral example for all things right and honorable isn't close to the level it needs to be. And we wonder why Dead Christians refuse to keep attending dead churches.

Let's be honest, as I discussed in the previous chapter, your ability to even read this book places you at an intellectual level far greater than the level of millions in our world. With the advances in technology, information can literally travel at the speed of one click. What this has done, in consequence, is raised the level of expectation of 'ministry'. No longer can a religious leader tell their parishioners what to do without receiving a who, when, where or why response. There was a time in history where the church was the place to receive information. In history, certain cultures depended on the religious leader to educate them about certain elements of life. The religious leader was considered the wise one. When education was scarce, one of the most revered positions was that of the Pastor. In present day, there are people that attend church with neuroscience engineering degrees. Yet Pastors, and religious leaders, still believe that a 'call' from God is what will earn them the respect of the community.

Can we face the fact Christians have become "too smart" to be a part of an ignorant community (church)?

When I think about the number of Dead Christians I have come in contact with, the truth is that many of them are intellectually alive. The truth is that the local church may stimulate their emotions, however True Christians are seeking something that will take them to a new level of excellence in their moral life. The era of "do it because the Bible says so" is dead. People are looking for the type of faith that will challenge them into aliveness. True Christians are searching for a place that will enlighten them and challenge them to become moral agents and not just church attendees.

People want to be a part of a faith system that gives them a call to action. I have a friend who doesn't attend church but is committed to giving financially to causes that better the community. Unfortunately, a small percentage of his money makes it into the church offering plate. He knows his giving won't make it to the causes he is passionate about. People don't just want to feel good on Sunday mornings. People want to connect with the communities they live in. What better feeling does a person get to know they improved a social disparity? By the time the Dead Christian reaches Wednesday night, they need another pick-me-up. The True Christian remains spiritually high all week because they are connected to something bigger than themselves. What I have noticed in my years of service is that people who serve with me keep their "high" longer than the Dead Christian. What I mean is when people serve once they become anxious to serve again!

Most people can experience, and become overwhelmed by too much worship. I have yet to meet a person who gets overwhelmed about service.

Think about it. You can ask a person to attend worship with you and their response will either be, "sure" or "I've already been." In most cases when you ask someone to serve, whether they just returned from a mission's trip in Haiti or not, the answer will often be in the affirmative. If nothing else the person will inquire more about the opportunity instead of giving an automatic decline. This is the reason I always invite people to serve at The Worship Center more than I ask them to come to one of our many worship environments. Serving keeps people moving. Serving keeps people excited about their Christianity. Service makes people want to do more and connect; because they feel like they are a part of something that is bigger than themselves.

I remember one commentary writing to the church, *"You don't matter. Churches that ignore the world aren't giving us any context for spirituality. Jesus walked in a world with political, social, economic, and spiritual forces at play. We, too, walk in a world with all of these forces. Jesus engaged them."* (Unknown, 2015) I believe we should engage these human dynamics as well. I believe we should be Christians that are actively involved, just like Jesus was, in political, social, economic and spiritual issues. I believe Christians, if no one else, because we profess to have the highest level of moral obligation, should be on the front line to champion certain issues.

Hearing the Heartbeat of God

Humanity is listening for the heartbeat of God. Humanity is seeking God's presence here on earth. Humanity wants to feel the pulse of generosity and kindness present in the everyday happenings of life. Humanity is looking for a moral example of right living and selfless care. Humanity wants to connect to the heart of God. True Christians should have the desire to be the heartbeat of God.

History continues to unfold itself. Along with that, history continues to repeat itself. It continues to repeat the disparities of humankind. It continues to repeat the cycle of oppression and classism. It continues to repeat economic inequality. However, with the repetition of all things mentioned, something else simultaneously repeats itself. The cries of children who have become victims of sex trafficking. The cries of people living with HIV who have been outcast by their families and society. The cries of felons who are looking for a fresh start in society. The cries of humanity for world peace and a better life for all mankind. While history repeats itself with disparity, humanity continues to cry out for hope. Humanity wants to hear the heartbeat of God in the world.

It is easy to be the hands and feet of God. It is easy to do service related activities on behalf of God. It is easy to give, and to serve, spontaneously. It is easy for a person to motivate and excite another person to give. But how many True Christians will make it a point to adopt service as a lifestyle? How many Dead Christians will push themselves to serve on more occasions than just Thanksgiving and Christmas? The truth of the matter is the heartbeat of God should have a consistent sound in humanity; displayed by the actions of True Christians worldwide.

There is a pulse in life. The same way in which blood flows through the heart of the human body, humanitarian acts should pour through the DNA of the globe. Every continent, every community, every class, every family, every gender, every human is connected, in some way, to this web of the world. One element of Christ Consciousness is to understand that we are all linked to a larger cosmic energy (God). At whatever point in history this book is being read I can guarantee there is a pulse in the world.

Maybe the pulse is directing our attention to police brutality and murder. Maybe the pulse is directing our attention to the political campaigns and government agendas. Maybe the pulse is directing our attention to the lack of food in Somalia. Maybe the pulse is drawing our attention to the lack of clean running water in Ghana. Perhaps the pulse is drawing our attention to the terroristic actions of a group of people. Regardless of time, there is a pulse present.

Medical studies say blood will always flow to the areas of the body that need the greatest attention. Where will the service of Christians flow in humanity?

The problem I see with most Dead Christians is instead of being selfless they have become self-serving. Dead Christians get excited about building buildings, church anniversaries, Pastor Anniversaries and launching satellite locations, but won't show their support or presence to Town Hall meetings about HIV, community summits surrounding sex trafficking, or open their facilities for homeless services. The love of God wants to flow, but there could possibly be a blood clot in the body of Christ.

Have we forgotten the message and model of Jesus? "For even the Son of Man did not come to be served, but to serve, and to give his life a ransom for many." Mark 10:45 NIV Often times I think to myself that if Jesus were alive today how would He view Christians? How would Jesus feel about the world's mindset of entitlement and narcissism? Jesus, of all people, was the "Son of God". If society should have treated anyone with royal treatment Jesus would have been the prime candidate.

Yet when we look at the model and ministry of Jesus we don't see him sitting at the head of the table too often. Where we often find Jesus is sitting on the floors of people's houses having an 'everyday' meal. The fact remains that much of the conflict surrounding Jesus was based on the element that he DID NOT solicit the royal treatment some thought he deserved. Yet Dead Christians have made their "walk with Christ" an observation sport. Dead Christians watch the world decay, yet have no conviction in their role for it's deterioration. The Jesus model was a method that touched the weaknesses of society and brought strength to the broken hearted. What Dead Christians have done is taken that model and packaged the message for "Religious Recruitment". Dead Christians have mastered bringing people in, but failed in places a wedge in the revolving door of church.

What we can learn from the life of Jesus is that God's heartbeat can only be heard if we place our service in the noisy environments of the marginalized. It is not merely in the "still small voice" that God makes His presence known to the world. In some cases it is in those "still small actions" that awaken the consciousness of others to know that God is still present on earth. Amidst the calamities of society, it's the small random acts of kindness and service that help others receive hope in a better world.

One of the key elements I believe Dead Christians are unwilling to swallow, with the responsibility of service, is the aspect of becoming a "ransom for many". As a Pastor who is leading the charge for more Christians in service to humanity, I can attest to the discomfort of being that ransom. By definition a ransom is a 'value put up in place for the freedom of something else'. Personal sacrifice is at the heart of human service. True Christians understand service requires personal time. Serving requires personal resources. Serving requires getting out of the comfort of a warm bed to serve the homeless in the snow. Serving requires your phone to ring at 1am to hear the voice of a teenager who wants to get out of the sex trade. Serving requires going to the first interview with a felon in order to vouch for their integrity and character.

In other words, it will cost you something personally to provide liberty and freedom for another.

It is unfortunate to say many Dead Christians will never get to this point of personal sacrifice. Most Dead Christians have no idea they are connected to things that are not "Christian". There is a lie that has been told to the world: *the sacred and the secular are separate.* This is a falsehood. I believe the moment Dead Christians see they are connected with the marginalized is the moment they will see the importance of service.

It is untrue to say the person living with HIV, the woman who is caught in the sex trafficking business and the town lacking clean running water have no connection to the Christian faith. The commonality is that these are the situations we are called to 'go' and address. The truth is these things are a part of our human existence, which can't be separated from our Christian existence. I blame the colonization era for this perpetuation of lies. This era of time initiated the "let US go help THEM" mentality.

Instead our mindset should be
"let US help and care for US"!

The bible supports this concept I like to call 'the other as me'. The scriptures tell us, *"In your relationships with one another, have the same mindset as Christ Jesus: Who, being in very nature God, did not consider equality with God something to be used to his own advantage; rather, he made himself nothing by taking the very nature of a servant, being made in human likeness."* Philippians 2:5-7 NIV The embodiment of God in human form was the ultimate display of God connecting with humanity. In the same way, we must learn to embody the plight of the marginalized as our own. We cannot wait until the misfortune "hits home" when we all share this geographic body called earth. We can't wear, with pride, our Christian hats and t-shirts when there are still men, women and children who heads and bodies are cold from their winters of sleeping on the streets. We can't keep pushing our bible teachings on 'Jesus as the living water' when there are still countries that don't have access to uncontaminated running water. If God can come to earth in human likeness, True Christians can present themselves in the world as equal and not superior. If Gods desire was to feel humanity, a True Christians desire should be to feel the pains of the oppressed, downtrodden and marginalized.

If Jesus can humble himself to think of himself on the same level as humanity, then certainly we can as True Christians. The whole belief in Jesus is centered on the idea that God doesn't mind associating God's self with the totality of humankind. The issue found with most Dead Christians is they believe their "Christian" association separates them from the rest of humanity. The term "Christian" should actually spawn the opposite consciousness.

The association of "Christian" should connect the carrier of the brand with the responsibility of connecting with humanity as self.

Jesus himself began to engrain this message into his followers. What I believe Jesus was trying to turn our ears to was a very specific message of altruism. If we were to look at the teachings of Jesus we would be able to see much of what he taught had nothing to do with the church. Rather Jesus wanted to teach people how to be people. One particular scripture that comes to mind is found in the gospel of Mark. The text says, *"Sitting down, Jesus called the Twelve and said, 'Anyone who wants to be first must be the very last, and the servant of all." Mark 9:35 NIV* In this statement, Jesus was giving us the key to success: service. He showed us how to move to the top of the class and to the head of the table. This principle is very evident in today's culture. Think of some of the most successful persons in the world. Then consider how much of their success is connected to their service and philanthropic efforts. Think about the large foundations they fund, give to, and have created. The reality is God blesses those who choose to bless others.

Jesus articulates to us to be people of provision. Jesus' message pushes us to the point where we have to reconsider what our true purpose is as human, and not necessarily as Dead Christian. Jesus declares to literally place ourselves at the back of the line and to contemplate placing the needs of others ahead of our own. This particular scripture also gives True Christians the assignment to care for all! While we as individuals can't touch every aspect of humanity we should be willing to touch the broad base of the world at the level that leaves no one excluded.

The actuality is we all have been given liberty and freedom in life. We all can attest to the point that we have come from a place of oppression. While some may not have had the situations of another, it is true no one starts at the top. Each of us, through the grace and mercy of God, have risen to the levels we find ourselves today. But how many of us have forgotten to consider those whose journey out of oppression is much more of a challenge than ours? Despite the fact I lived in a state of homelessness for almost a year, the process it took for me was much shorter than those I come in contact with each week on the streets of Atlanta. I have been arrested for a felony, however my process of going through the judicial system was much quicker than others. My point is we have all been in the darkness and made our way to the light. For those who are still experiencing their process, we must be patient as they complete their journey.

We should be willing to help others find the same liberty and freedom we have been graced. We should live our lives in such a way where we don't get relaxed with our fortune to the point we forget about the misfortunes of others. The scriptures even tell us, *"You, my brothers and sisters, were called to be free. But do not use your freedom to indulge the flesh; rather, serve one another humbly in love" Galatians 5:13 NIV* True Christians know they have been given their freedom for the purpose of helping others. Dead Christians are those who see their liberty as a blessing but have turned a blind eye to the oppression of others.

The free and the oppressed have much in common. But the free will never admit this truth until they are willing to relate and touch the needs of the oppressed. Whenever people come out to feed the homeless with The Worship Center there is this continued consciousness and observation made by all our volunteers; the people in the line receiving food look no different from those in the line giving the meals.

True Christians are comfortable with the statement there is nothing that separates the Jew from the Gentile, the homeless from the mansion owner, the single mother from the married with child woman, the person living with HIV from the person in perfect health. The bible paints for us the picture for what true community should look like, *"Everyone was filled with awe at the many wonders and signs performed by the apostles. All the believers were together and had everything in common. They sold property and possessions to give to anyone who had need"* Acts 2:43-45 NIV Let's be genuine, most Dead Christians have more than enough to take care of what they need in life. True Christians understand their overflow should be used in order to help the poor and the oppressed.

Becoming the Heartbeat of God

If Dead Christians want to become people who are relevant we must primarily become people that are relational. But not relational in the element of engaging people, we must be willing to engage the social issues. One of the primary displays of Jesus' ministry was centered on Social Justice. If True Christians want to truly become the heartbeat of God we must be willing to go deep into the environments and areas of the marginalized that Jesus made himself present in.

The heart is located deep in the rib cage. Therefore, the heartbeat is located deep in the anatomy of the human body. Utilizing this same analogy, the heart of God is located deep in the center of social issues and injustices. Likewise, the sound of God's heart should be positioned deep in the anatomy of Christian service. Becoming the heartbeat of God is determined by where we place ourselves in the body of mankind. The heart, because of what flows through it, connects every organ, muscle, tissue and atom in the body. The same holds true for True Christians. Because of the message that flows through the gospel, True Christians have the ability to connect communities and environments. In the same way Jesus enlightened us to a new consciousness through Old Testament thought, we now have the responsibility to expand New Testament thought in order to enlighten present day thinkers.

The Prophet Isaiah maps out our responsibility as Christians inside of his prophetic writings. Isaiah 1:17 reads, *"Learn to do good; seek justice, correct oppression; bring justice to the fatherless, plead the widow's case."* The most challenging part of this text is located beyond the first four words. We are all taught as children to do good. One of the primary messages of the Christian faith is to do good. Doing good is easy. It is easy to identify 'good things' a person can do with their lives and for others. It is easy to give your time and money to projects as good deeds. True Christians will read this text in its totality and make the cognizant decision to exercise every element of the author's words. A True Christian won't stop at "Learn to do good".

Unfortunately, just being a Good Christian will turn you into a Dead Christian.

It's what we read beyond "Learn to do good" that requires True Christians to engage with humanity and get dirty! In order to seek justice we must go looking for opportunities that need our moral compass. It has always amazed me at the level of resources the church and Christians have, yet we have to be propositioned before doing anything with those resources. Why can't Christians be the ones running to the front line for service? Why are we not banging down the doors of organizations and initiatives to discover their needs?

Some may be curious as to why my views towards Christians have become so critical. The truth is that it has nothing to do with Christian actions. It is actually connected with Dead Christians non-action on issues. From my current perspective I know there are countless organizations and movements who have requested the help and partnership of churches only to be told at the front desk, "we already have something like that here" by the church receptionist.

As the biblical writing states, it is our responsibility to "correct oppression" and "bring justice". I am of the personal belief many Dead Christians are afraid to correct oppression because we are too afraid to call out the oppressor! Many Dead

Christians are fearful to usher in justice for all. This process would entail bucking and demolishing the systems that perpetuate the injustices. It will take courage to accomplish these tasks, but what better soldier for humanity than a soldier for God.

There are some major elements I believe Jesus wanted each of us to consider. We should consider these recommendations not as our Christian duty, but as our human obligation. Even if you do not identify yourself as a Christian, or person of religious affiliation, there should be some moral pull on your consciousness to do good for others.

Jesus was calling True Christians to action. We cannot define ourselves as Christians if we are not on the move. One consistency in Jesus' ministry was that he was always on the move. He traveled from city to city because he understood the bigness of his mission. Jesus understood that a true example of being God's heartbeat on earth would require action and momentum. I believe Jesus was frustrated with the 'word' of the synagogue and wanted to see people acting out the gospel. To the same point, I believe people are tired of hearing the talk of Christians and want to see Christians walk the walk they profess. What Jesus saw in bible days, I believe, has only perpetuated itself in modern day: idle people. Jesus championed a call to action during his time on earth. I would like to do the same! **I am calling True Christians from their places of idleness and challenging them to act on the issues that still plague humanity.**

It is interesting to note when we see Jesus interacting with religious leaders and magistrates they often challenged him with the written text. Jesus' reply would always call people to act on what they were taught. Jesus also challenged the thinkers of the day to re-evaluate how they did ministry. Jesus created a movement while Dead Christians became comfortable with studying and learning about His words. If we are going to be true Christians we must be willing to move into the areas and environments that need our action and support. It never ceases to amaze me the number of Christians who are content sitting in the chairs of church with no desire to get up and walk into humanity as game changers.

Dead Christians can tell you what the bible says. Dead Christians can tell you what the Pastor preached on Sunday (if they weren't sleep). Dead Christian can tell you how to live right. Dead Christians can give you the dos and the don'ts of life. Dead

Christians can quote litanies and hymns. Dead Christians will always be present in vacation bible school. Dead Christians will always be present in bible study and Sunday morning worship. Comparable to bible days, Dead Christians will always be in the synagogue reading the scribes. However, when will True Christians choose to show up in the same environments of the oppressed and the marginalized?

Jesus was a human who championed social justice. The primary message of Jesus was to raise the awareness of social issues. Outside of Jesus' believed divinity and miracle workings, we cannot throw out the fact that Jesus was a human who advocated for change and communal fairness. Jesus saw, even in his era, that were was a need for a voice that advocated for the marginalized and the disenfranchised. Jesus took the lead when others were afraid. From the story of the Good Samaritan to the woman who was caught in adultery, Jesus identified the wrongs of the world and gave recommendations for a new way of human agency. His example was out of the norm. Jesus not only showed he was connected to the people, he also demonstrated through his words his feelings about some of the social dynamics in his city.

As a Rabbi, or religious teacher, Jesus was well aware of the law and how it would be executed. Jesus was well aware that his actions would stir up concern and dissatisfaction from the church. Jesus was well versed on the divide between communities and classes. Jesus was cognizant of his interactions with the poor, the adulterer, the prostitute, the fisherman and the tax collector. Jesus knew that "his kind" wasn't to associate with the communities listed above. Nevertheless Jesus realized His voice had the power to shift the nations and to change the consciousness of the world. It is a shame other religious leaders, who have innumerable ears at their attention each week, refuse to use their platform to inform the masses about the inequalities that are still prevalent in the world.

Historically speaking, a person cannot negate why Jesus was killed. Christians have come to believe Jesus' death was for salvation and their sins. We have also come to believe that Jesus was killed because of his religious teachings and miracles. While these philosophies are valid in their own right, the truth is that Jesus was processed through the judicial system for his stance on government and the church's involvement in social issues. Jesus was killed because He was shifting the norm and calling out the wrongs of humanity.

Jesus was a trouble maker. Jesus wasn't liked. But then it wasn't just for what He did, it was a matter of what He said. If we are going to be champions for social justice, as Jesus was, we cannot be afraid to utilize our voices. We can't be so focused on doing a good deed that we forget to dialogue with the environments to which the good deed is being executed. Change doesn't take place exclusively through the actions of a community. True change happens when leaders, and other influential persons, get together and begin dialogue about a process involving an implementation strategy for solutions.

Jesus died because Jesus was creating societal change; not because he was building a church.

Jesus believed in equality. Jesus was the personification of God meeting people on their level. Jesus, as the Son of God, hung out with the "least of them". God incarnate came to earth to prove that, even He, can humble Himself to be equal (on the same level) as man. The problem Jesus had with the environment he lived in was the hierarchal system that was tearing humanity apart. Jesus was tired of people thinking of themselves as higher than the humility of God.

No two people are the same. To the same degree no two people carry the same qualifications for all environments. This does not mean we have to view someone else as other than human. Jesus' greatest tension was trying to understand why people were viewed so differently when we are all, at the core, human. Equality does not mean everyone necessarily being the same and on the same level. What equality means is that each person should be placed on the same level of **value** as the other. Jesus never advocated that everyone should be the same. Jesus gave a compelling example of how everyone should be **treated** the same; with love and dignity.

Society created the pods of magistrates, Sadducees, Pharisees, Priest, tax collectors, prostitutes and the sick. It has been made evident in the scriptures that each of these pods had their own communities. What can be observed in history is that there was to be no comingling between any of these groups. **Jesus breaks the system of inequality by inviting everyone to eat at the same table.** When you examine the occupations of the twelve disciples you will discover that Jesus was trying to get us to understand no person has more, or greater value, than another person. Jesus' inner circle of followers were a mix-match gathering of people.

When will we be like Jesus and invite the fisherman, the tax collector, the bookkeeper and the Zealot together? When will we be like Jesus and invite the Muslim, the single mother, the prostitute, the person living with HIV and the felon to the same table to eat?

Jesus believed that social issues are real issues. Jesus' message challenges us not to separate ourselves from, what I would like to call, "the other". The issue I find with most Dead Christians is they are focused on the wrong issues. I would almost venture to say that Dead Christians aren't focused on any issues at all. Christianity has become one of those things that has caused many people, after joining a church or a fellowship, to put much of their attention into the four walls of the building. Most Dead Christians focus on what their church is doing in their community with their resources led by their Pastor/Leader.

I believe Jesus' message to the world was for us to focus on humanitarian and global issues. We cannot turn a blind eye to the lack of clean water in Ghana as a result of our focus on our soup kitchen in Atlanta. We cannot turn a deaf ear to the cries of children being sold as sex slaves in Brazil because we are too focused on implementing our new Vacation Bible School

Curriculum in Baltimore. We can't miss the need to provide food for the homeless because we are focused on the Pastor's Anniversary Banquet. We cannot forget to support the single mother who is living away from her family because we are focused on the next church musical.

Social issues are the real issues we should be grabbing by the bull's horn and riding until our palms are bloody.

True Christians should begin the process of "focus inversion" in the church. Instead of the lens centering to the altar of the sanctuary, we should be out building altars (places that suggest the presence of God) outside the church. The attention of the Christian should be far from meeting budgets and planning conferences. Instead, it should be on community agendas and global solution discoveries. The True Christians voice can't just be heard in the pulpits; it should be heard on the steps of City Hall. Dead Christians like fads and buzz words. True Christians hear the genuine issues and refuse to cease dialogue until solutions are not just brought to the table but implemented. The real issues of Christianity are not religious, or faith, issues at all. The true issues for the True Christian are philanthropic.

Jesus believed in human rights over political rights. Jesus believed that human rights and global justice should be harmonious. As I stated before, Jesus was killed because of his conscious-raising actions towards the government. This is what would label him an advocate. I would suggest every miracle Jesus performed was preceded by a statement of human rights. Jesus had the mentality, and voice, that spoke "All have the same value as the other". Jesus' message always challenged the idea that even the least are deserving of redemption.

While history and communities have always advocated for the separation of church and state, Jesus demonstrated to us a different ideal. Yes, God's law and man's law can remain separate. However, separate does not mean disassociation. One's decisions reflect directly on the other. What Jesus showed us is that while the laws can remain separate there can still be dialogue across party lines. What Jesus teaches us is that the priest and the president should be seated at the same table. In order to form better communities, there needs to be a moral element partnered with a system of checks and balances. There should be leadership in place that can uphold the laws of the land as well as uphold an ethical standard for humanity. Jesus was never against government. In truth, Jesus advises us to honor government officials and to revere them as elected by God. What Jesus did not agree with was the "government of the church". What he saw was people who thought themselves above the law and wanted to be "God's Judges" here on earth.

Jesus utilized his voice to make sure all were treated as human. The message I believe Jesus wanted each of us to model was that there is no government system, or otherwise, that can place value on an individual. We are all God's children, and because of that we should all be treated with the highest esteem and regard.

Please do not misinterpret my exegesis of the biblical scriptures. Jesus did believe Government should be in place and that all government has been ordained by God. There is a difference in the implementation of rules and regulations by government; and government determining who has access to certain rights and who doesn't. I believe Jesus' message addressed the latter of the two. We cannot identify what "human rights" are until we come the understanding of what "human" is. We cannot keep pushing social and community issues until we have a clear Christ Consciousness about our responsibility to the person.

Jesus was a man for the oppressed. It is easy for us to point the finger at the current social issues happening in our world. But how many Dead Christians are taking that same finger and adding more pressure to the oppressed situations.

There can be no oppression if there is no oppressor.

Jesus refused to be a part of the problem. As Christians, we should also refuse to add to the situational oppression of others. From the days of Moses, until now, we have witnessed a God of the oppressed. Over the course of history it has been clear that God hears the cries of the oppressed. Throughout time we have seen God reveal God's self in the form of liberator for the people. If the term "Messiah" translates as the "promised deliverer" one should pose the question 'to whom does the Messiah come to deliverer'? What has happened over the ages is we have forgotten the true purpose, and need, of God. Humanity cannot save itself. Humanity needs the energy from which it was birthed for redemption. Yet, God thrives off the participation of human agency in the world. Unfortunately, what happened in the days of Moses has reoccurred in the modern day Christendom.

What has happened over the course of history is Dead Christians have become the oppressors. Placing judgement on the marginalized is just as immoral as the actions of the person who created the margin. From the days of Moses, and the Exodus story, we have always seen God as a God of the oppressed. We have always seen a God who has a heart for the oppressed. History has shown us oppressed communities and people are the communities and people who need the most compassion.

When we see the oppressed we should not see an opportunity to get 'Christian brownie points'. When we see the oppressed we should not see a photo op situation. When we see the oppressed we should not see a chance to look like the Super Man/Woman of the day. When we see the oppressed we should not see an opportunity to make ourselves feel better about our lives. Caring for, and tending to the needs of the oppressed, is about answering the question, "How can the love of God be displayed in this environment?" What True Christians bring to the oppressed environments is hope. True Christians have been commissioned to plant seeds in our community that produce the fruits of the spirit: Love, Joy, Peace, Patience, Kindness, Goodness, Faithfulness, Gentleness and Self-Control (Galatians 5:22-23).

Why have Christians not taken the lead in demonstrating compassion to the modern day oppressed community? The truth is we have identified these communities, however our hearts do not bleed for them. Outside of the oppressed communities I have listed in this text, there are many other pods of people who suffer from oppression on a daily basis. The component that makes my heart bleed is how Dead Christians have ostracized the oppressed from the community of believers.

If we are going to exhibit the heartbeat of God we have to be Christians who have compassion towards those who have been cast aside by others. Will we become a people that relieves the pressure of the oppressed instead of adding weight to the system?

Jesus and the disinherited. So often are their people in society that were once a part of the 'inner circle'. Yet one small change in their status caused them to be pushed outside of the circle. We have all made mistakes in life. However, Dead Christians, and society, have labeled some situations as non-redemptive. There are communities of people who were a part of the family who now have become the disinherited.

I am always shocked at the issues, and communities of people, Dead Christians refuse to touch and engage. One thing we pride ourselves with at The Worship Center is our willingness to go into the 'dark corners' of ministry. We are comfortable going into communities where others have turned the street lights off. I've stated before that much of Jesus' footsteps can be traced in the 'ghettos' of Jerusalem. At one point in my ministry I was afraid of certain communities and how they would treat me as 'not one of them'. But I soon realized the greatest hurt I could have done to those communities of people was to leave them to fend for themselves; to leave them with no hope and no love. There are numerous communities who need the most hope and love, yet receive the least attention.

I come in contact with countless persons throughout the year who are so appreciative of the fact that someone cared enough to show them love. Every month I shake the hands of homeless persons in Atlanta who say, "Pastor we appreciate what you do for us". I walk to the doors of senior citizens in our county who receive Meals on Wheels to hear the words, "young man thank you; please place the box on the counter." I have walked the streets of Atlanta at 9pm on a Friday to hear a young woman say, "I don't like selling my body, but I have to. Thank you for praying with me." On the first Sunday of each month I hear, "Pastor its great you provide Free HIV testing for those who can't afford it". I have seen the eyes of a community light up when their new water purification system produces its first few pints of water. People want to know they matter. People want to know they are cared for. People want to know someone out there thinks more about others than they think about themselves.

The felon is worthy of redemption. Their one legal mistake, or multiple, judicial run ins do not disqualify them from the compassion of the Christian community. The single mother, who only has evidence of what other non-married Christians do behind closed doors, is still worthy of being embraced by the community she grew up in. The Homeless, who like many of us were just one check away from poverty, do not deserve to be ignored. The person living with HIV, whether sexually transmitted or by medical mistake, should not be viewed as the leper of biblical times. The person who is same gender loving deserves to be loved as they are, regardless if you agree with their lifestyle or not. The woman who sleeps with men for money, although some of these men are active in our churches, deserves not to be looked at as if her 'mistake' is unforgivable.

These are just a few examples of people God is challenging us to embrace. If anything, these are the ones who need Christ's love showered on them the most. These are those who need forgiveness the most. These are those in need of compassion. But what true Christians should offer this group of people is an opportunity, and environment, for redemption.

Jesus connected with the disenfranchised. Jesus connected with those who we were taught to distance ourselves from. Let's be honest. Some of the above mentioned classes of people we have been trained to disassociate from. *Much of this perpetuated action I blame on those who carry the privilege of the platform.* I blame those who have the voice, and have the audiences, for the continued stigmas that are echoed in our community. I blame those who preach condemnation and not forgiveness. I blame those who speak about wrong but will never promote the "right thing to do".

The issue with the Dead Christian is they do not embrace the ought of life. The actions we ought to be taking to reconcile and connect the disenfranchised back to Christ. This entire text is centered on the oughts of Christianity. Listed on these pages are the things we, as True Christians, ought to be doing.

Jesus understood that to look at 'the other' was to look in the eyes of God. Jesus said, *"For I was hungry and you gave me food, I was thirsty and you gave me drink, I was a stranger and you welcomed me, I was naked and you clothed me, I was sick and you visited me, I was in prison and you came to me."* (Matthew 25:35-36 ESV) Taking care of the needs of humanity is taking care of Christ. Everything a true Christian does should feel like their responsibility to God's self.

Jesus advocated for the greatest since of community. If you could collect all of Jesus' message into one phrase what could you come up with? I would say, "Humanity that lives as one". The prophetic writings proclaimed the messiah would be one who would usher in global peace. While Jesus didn't directly accomplish this in his lifetime, his message, however, pointed us in the direction of a global community that lives in harmony with one another.

What I believe Jesus wanted to enlighten us on was a global consciousness of the African Proverb 'I am because you are'. This age-old proverb is still displayed in current day African derived religions and cultures. People still look out for one another in the same way they would look out for themselves. We too should strive for this example of communal living.

If we were to dissect the ministry of Jesus it would slap us in the face with this principle. Jesus was a strong activist for connecting people back to God and humanity. What we can learn from the model of Jesus is that we have been guilty of creating these pockets of separation. What we have not come to the realization of is that the creation of these pods is what has been killing the faith community.

How do we begin this process of displaying God's love as service to humanity?

Jesus, and the Prophet Isaiah, state the same authoritative words in the bible. *"The spirit of the Lord is upon me, because he has anointed me to proclaim good news to the poor. He has sent me to proclaim liberty to the captives and recovering of sight to the blind, to set at liberty those who are oppressed, to proclaim the year of the Lord's favor." (Luke 4:18, Isaiah 61:1)* These commanding words offer to True Christians an excellent point of departure for service. These words became the quintessential connection between the Old and the New Testament. In the same regard, I believe these words can help us to connect the New Testament with present day culture. Jesus did it as He often quoted the messages of the prophet in his teaching. Now we must take Jesus' message and ensure it is being carried properly until His return.

The heart beat must proclaim good news to the poor.
We have to begin utilizing the power of our voices. What True Christians should embrace is the art of advocacy and activism. Coupled with advocacy is the awareness and new sense of consciousness needed surrounding the issues. There are a plethora of social justice issues which require our attention. But how are we supposed to know what they are if there is no one out there bringing awareness to them?

The certainty is it would be foolish for one person to attempt having their hands in all the items listed in this text. One person cannot save humanity. While there should be specific things we are involved in, we can champion our voices to as many causes as our mouths will allow. What we can see in the life and ministry of Jesus is His voice as it called for the awareness of injustices.

What we see throughout the biblical text is Jesus bringing a new sense of realization to the issues people of his time chose to turn a blind eye to. What we can learn from Jesus' example is just because the issue doesn't affect you personally, doesn't mean the issue doesn't require our attention communally. Most Dead Christians live with the mentality of "I'm not going through it and no one I know is going through it". But what happens when you DO go through it and seek the compassion of other Dead Christians like yourself? Do we understand the cycle of selfishness we are perpetuating?

The heartbeat must attend to the poor. The True Christian's efforts should be altruistic. True Christians are selfless. Dead Christians are selfish and are unconscious of the 'richness' God has blessed them with. I believe when we are first exposed to the word poor we automatically think it means to not have money or material goods. What I believe the word 'poor' should point our attention to those who ultimately need hope.

There are so many things God has graced humanity with. One of the foremost messages I believe humanity should carry to others is that life is the greatest blessing. Life, each day, gives us an awareness that we still have purpose.

The poor doesn't need handouts, they need hope.

Humans are, by nature, selfish. It takes exposure and enlightenment for a person to learn selflessness. We have been taught since we were young to always look out for ourselves. We are even told when traveling, that in the event of an emergency to place personal safety above the safety of others. What would happen if we lived in a world that wasn't created through the 'survival of the fittest' mentality? We should learn, as True Christians, how to take care of something other than ourselves.

The heartbeat's ultimate goal should be liberty. Our action's end result should be freedom for all. Dead Christians have become blind to the suppression experienced throughout humanity. Those that are suffering in society have become prisoners to their conditions. What true Christians should promote is the actuality that all have the potential of being liberated from their present environment.

The felon deserves liberty from being perceived as a criminal after they have served their time. The single mother deserves liberty from being judged for having a child unmarried. The person living with HIV deserves liberty from being viewed as unclean and dirty because of their health status. The person living under the condition of homelessness deserves liberty from being assumed as a drunk, a drug addict or a mentally ill person.

Not only society, but Dead Christians have created these prisons that do not appreciate the autonomous value of the individual. However, many of these prisons were erected through the ignorance of people. What Dead Christians have done is perpetuated how they were taught to interact with these groups. The reality is many of us were taught to interact with oppressed communities by separating ourselves from them. Instead of engaging, we were trained to disassociate ourselves. Not only did we place a wall between us and them, but what we ultimately created was societal prison cells that only marginalized the ones we have been created to serve.

It only takes four walls to create a room. Therefore it only takes four Dead Christians to reject a group into isolation.

The heartbeat should touch the captives. The process of introducing captives back into society requires restoration and redemption. The issue I find with most Dead Christians is they forget about their process of redemption and restoration. It is amazing to me how Dead Christians won't go to the degree of actually walking with the oppressed. The attitude of "just give them Jesus and let them figure it out" is killing humanity. True Christians should be willing to matriculate through these processes in order to produce a whole, and restored, human being.

There must be a system which tends to the needs of the person. What do I mean by tending to the needs of the person? It's simple. We as True Christians should be the like parents holding on to the back seat of the oppress' bicycle. It is hard for a 3 year old learning how to ride a bike without the support of their guardian. In like manner, it is a challenge for the oppressed to find their footing in society without the support of the community. It is so disheartening to me at how churches will give out bibles and worship marketing material, but are unwilling to make the journey with the person.

The levels of restoration and redemption should give the oppressed intrinsic and autonomous value that's within. The key to true ministry and outreach is to promote the worth of an individual beyond their present environment. The focus of True Christians should be to campaign to others for the rights and privileges of the burdened. The focus should also be to speak to the oppressed in such a way that affirms their personhood and value.

The heartbeat should provide healing. Nevertheless we must understand healing within itself is a process. As I stated in the previous section, our mission as True Christians is to introduce the mentality of **process healing** and not **instant healing**. When a person hears the term healing, a Dead Christian would automatically associate it with physical sickness. But when the bible speaks about healing, True Christians will understand that any broken aspect of life, or our world, requires healing.

Broken relationships. Broken finances. Broken career paths. Broken families and homes. Broken educational pursuits. There are countless things in life that will leave a person broken. While it doesn't take long, or much, to break a person, it is a process to heal from whatever broke them. True Christians will learn to bring a positive spiritual aspect to this process.

In the same manner a cut heals on the physical body, likewise we should embrace the healing process of the oppressed and humanity. Healing often happens in stages and in layers. Taking this information into consideration, we must remain

121

sensitive to the various levels we may find the oppressed. We have to recognize there are some who have recently fallen into their state of oppression. We have to recognize there are people who have just begun their journey of restoration. We should be thoughtful of the various stages each person is experiencing.

The heartbeat should be aimed in the direction of the oppressed. In the same esteem as healing, eradicating oppressive behavior must be implicit as a process. Oppression doesn't happen overnight. Over time people fall into oppressed states. Over time people develop stereotypes and stigmas about oppressed people. Over time society tries to remedy oppression. What we should understand as True Christians, is in order to liberate someone from oppression we must be willing to walk with others in their journey out of oppression. We should be humans who care about the rising up of people out of oppressed states. However, we must also note that the rising action is a process within itself.

The first step is relieving the pressure Dead Christians have placed in the system. Over time Dead Christians have become the issuc. Over time Dead Christians have only added to the problem of oppression. Over time Dead Christians have made the weight heavier on those who are trying to get a leg up. Dead Christians do this with their judgements and stereotypes. I introduced a concept to a friend of mine to end homelessness in the Atlanta area, their initial response was, 'so how do we make sure they don't sell drugs in the houses?'. How have we become so ignorant to still make assumptions that all homeless people sell drugs, are mentally ill or substance abusers? I was expecting his response to be, 'Pastor that's a great initiative! What do we have to do to make it happen?'

We wonder why the oppressed never rise? Dead Christians won't allow them to. We wonder why the homeless remain homeless? Because Dead Christians sill assume they are all on drugs or ex-convicts. We wonder why the felon will never find employment? Because Dead Christians still assume what they were arrested for is unforgivable; even after they have served their time. We wonder why the person living with HIV won't attend our worship experiences? Because Dead Christians are too afraid to touch them at the altar when they come for prayer. We wonder why poverty, human sex trafficking, drug wars and social injustices remain prevalent in the world? Because Dead Christians refuse to get involved in the remedy the problems.

If True Christians want to help the oppressed, our primary responsibility is to relieve their pressure.

The heartbeat must operate continuously as 'the year of the Lord'. To me this is the most important element of the scripture as it relations to Christ's message of Social Justice. We can talk about doing the work of God, or we can do the work of God. However, the work has to begin now. God's timing is now timing. Dead Christians have been waiting for someone else to do the work. True Christians should be on fire to initiate the movement now!

One practice I have adopted as a True Christian is to act when I see injustices being perpetrated. I understand I can't act on everything. On the other hand what I can do, I am unafraid to get involved with. What I have come to embrace is my role, and my part, in the problem. Will I be a part of the remedy, or will my silence only propagate the problem? A Dead Christian can blame ignorance to their noninvolvement with social issues. A True Christian, once they become aware of the cries of humanity, should have a new sense of accountability and responsibility.

Jesus' message for a change was a message of "action now". Jesus addressed issues and spoke truth to power in the moment injustices presented themselves. He spoke when others would have wanted him to be silent. Nevertheless, he spoke on behalf of the people whose voices would have never made it to the ears of those who had the influence to make change. Jesus did not just speak to the oppressed, He spoke for the oppressed.

Either we can be a people who wait, and talk, and meet, and plan, or we can be a people of action and change.

CLEAR! Resurrect the zombies!

Our time together is coming to a close. I pray, if nothing else, this text has made you more aware of the present issues that are happening around the globe. I pray the information in this text has, in some way, touched your heart to become active in the work that still must be done in humanity. It is my prayer you have a greater sense of responsibility; but more importantly you would hold yourself more accountable as a True Christian.

I wrote this text with the intent of reaching the present day human. But as I discussed in the previous chapter, the present day is now. Whether you are reading this text in 2015 or 2050 our responsibility remains the same: To serve the current needs of humanity.

My push isn't for you to go to church more. My push is not for you to read the bible more. My push is not for you to pray more. My push is not for you to meditate more. While these acts of faith, and practices, are a part of our religious journey, my push is for you to devote yourself to be the heartbeat of God here on earth. To be the hands, feet and representation of God's love, grace and mercy to humanity.

Let's be honest, if you are reading this book you are more than likely in the generational classification of the millennials. You were probably raised in church, or are constantly being told to go to church. But you don't attend church. It's not because you don't like church, or appreciate the spiritual necessity of worship, you just don't see the church doing what you believe they should be doing in the community and the globe. You would love to be connected to a church that feeds you spiritually. But then again you also desire a ministry that will allow you to work and serve humanity. *"Many people my age are simply not interested in church, organized religion or religion in general, and no number of projectors, hip, youthful pastors, or twitter hashtags are going to change that."* (Chiakulas, 2015) **You don't want to become a Dead Christian yourself.** You may be saying to yourself, "I miss church, but I have yet to find a ministry doing what I believe the church should be doing. I want to be involved. I also have not found a church that helps be to embrace my personal humanity and journey to enlightenment.

However, "I know from experience that there are huge numbers of millennials that are open to organized religion, and in fact are yearning from a church that they feel comfortable devoting their time and spiritual energy towards." (Chiakulas, 2015) I encounter people every day who are tired of churches that do nothing for the community. Instead of raising their concern to Pastors and church leadership, present day millennials have chosen to disassociate themselves from organized religion. However, after I launched The Worship Center in Atlanta I came across countless people who were desperately looking for opportunities to serve and give back. The zombies of Christianity are ready to receive life! But more importantly, humans are prepared to connect back to humanity!

True Christians are looking for a way to connect to the message of Jesus. True Christians are looking for a way to not just 'be' Christians, but for a way to do the work of Christ. True Christians have studied the bible for themselves and are appalled at how Dead Christians have contributed nothing to the world. True Christians have read the words of Jesus and are bold enough to do the courageous things Jesus did.

True Christians are Dead Christian who were tired of living but not giving life.

I was, like many of you, tired of the romanticized Jesus. I was tired of seeing Dead Christians at Thanksgiving and Christmas but never noticed them serving throughout the remainder of the year. I was tired of preachers preaching messages about grace, love, and forgiveness, but never teaching application and action. I was seeing church after church, ministry after ministry, and Dead Christian after Dead Christian doing nothing to eradicate the social injustices held in their own community, let alone with world. "Millennials are not interested in a celestial Jesus with a permanent smile and open arms, unconcerned with the goings-on of planet earth. We've heard about that Jesus our entire lives, and we're not buying it." (Chiakulas, 2015)

I stopped buying it, and in return started putting something else on the menu to offer True Christians.

"Do you know what we would buy? Jesus the man, Jesus the prophet, the Jesus that fashioned a whip of cords and overturned the tables of the money changers for making God's house a den of robbers. The Jesus that challenged the establishment and paid the ultimate price. The Jesus that took up the cross of the poor, the weak and the marginalized in the name of God" (Chiakulas, 2015) This is the type of Jesus the True

Christians desires to follow. This radical approach to human agency is consistent with the mentality of the present day millennial. The radical, the bold, the courageous, the dirty and marginalized desire this message of Jesus! You can't pull the wool over the eyes of True Christians the same way people have pulled the white sheet over the eyes of Dead Christians.

The problem with Christianity, and the church today, has nothing to do with the style of worship or the message of the church. Where the greatest rub takes place is how the message of Jesus manifests itself in the world. Dead Christians will attend church all day. Dead Christians will go to conferences all year. Dead Christians will stay at home and pray. Dead Christians will read books. Dead Christians will go to bible study. But True Christians will become God's human agents and act.

An internet blogger wrote, "I'm all for love and a personal relationship with God, but I choose to follow the man who teaches that political action is worship, that social justice is love." (Chiakulas, 2015) I've stated it consistently throughout this book. If certain issues, and the awareness of social injustices, do not move you into action you should turn in your Christian Card. There is much more to Christianity than communal worship and personal devotion. The primary reason the first Christians received the credibility they received was because of their social involvement.

There was one key event in history that Christians believed separated Jesus from all of the other prophets. It wasn't his words. It wasn't his actions. It wasn't his miracles. It wasn't even his death. The main event that separates Jesus from all the other prophets before him is the belief in his resurrection. What will separate True Christians from Dead Christians? It won't be their words. It won't be their involvement in worship experiences. It won't be the healings and deliverances. It will be their involvement, and resurrection, in the thread of humanity.

People are listening for the heartbeat of God.

People are looking for ways to connect back to God and humanity. The Question is much larger than "Dead Christians: Where is the Heartbeat of God". I believe if Dead Christians continue acting (or should I say non-acting) in the way they have been, the question will ultimately become "Where is God?"

References

Baily, S. P. (2015, May 12). *Christianity faces sharp decline as Americans are becoming even less affiliated with religion.* Retrieved from The Washington Post: www.washingtonpost.com/news/acts-of-faith/wp/2015/05/12/christianity-faces-sharp-decline-as-americans-are-becoming-even-less-affiliated-with-religion/

Center for Disease Control and Prevention. (2015, September 14). *Basic Statistics.* Retrieved from www.cdc.gov/hiv/statistics/basics.html

Centers for Disease Control and Prevention. (2015, June 5). *Global WASH Fast Facts.* Retrieved from www.cdc.gov/healthywater/global/wash_statistics.html

Chiakulas, C. (2015, September 30). *Churches could fill their pews with millennials if they just did this.* Retrieved from The Huffington Post: www.huffingtonpost.com/christian-chiakulas/churches-millennials-if-they-just-did-this_b_8215846.html

Do Something Organization. (n.d.). *11 Facts about Human Trafficking.* Retrieved from www.dosomething.org/facts/11-facts-about-human-trafficking

Ford, L. C. (2015, July 21). *Sex Trafficking: The New American slavery.* Retrieved from CNN News: www.cnn.com/2015/07/20/us/sex-trafficking/

Huffington Post. (2015, October 2). *The U. S. Illiteracy Rate Hasnt Changed in 10 Years.* Retrieved from www.huffingtonpost.com/2013/09/06/illiteracy-rate_n_3880355.html

Kilough, C. (2015). *Why is Christianity Becoming Irrelevant?* Retrieved from lifehopeandtruth.com: http://lifehopeandtruth.com/change/the-church/why-is-christianity-becoming-irrelevant/

National Alliance to End Homelessness. (2015, April 1). *The State of Homelessness in America 2015*. Retrieved from www.endhomelessness.org/library/entry/the-state-of-homelessness-in-america-2015

National Coalition Against Domestic Violence. (n.d.). *Statistics.* Retrieved from www.ncadv.org/learn/statistics

Nazworth, N. (2015, May 15). *CP U.S.* Retrieved from The Christian Post: www.christianpost.com/news/is-christian-decline-in-america-due-to-fewer-incognito-atheists-like-russsell-moore-said-cp-asked-pew-research-for-the-answer-139133/

Quigley, B. (2015, January 18). *10 Facts About Homelessness.* Retrieved from Economy In Crisis: www.economyincrisis.org/content/10-facts-about-homelessness

Stetzer, E. (2014, June). *3 Reasons People are not Involved in Your Church.* Retrieved from Christianity Today: http://www.christianitytoday.com/edstetzer/2014/june/3-reasons-people-are-not-involved-in-your-church.html

Unknown. (2015, October 13). *Here are 3 reasons no one is joining your church (plus one more).* Retrieved from Reluctant Xtian: www.reluctantxian.wordpress.com/2015/10/13/here-are-3-reasons-no-one-is-joining-your-church-plus-one-more

Vagianos, A. (2015, February 13). *30 Shocking Domestic Violence Statistics that Remins us its an epidemic.* Retrieved from Huff Post Women: www.huffingtonpost.com/2014/10/23/domestic-violence-statistics_n_5959776.html

Water.org. (n.d.). *Millions Lack Safe Water.* Retrieved from www.water.org/water-crisis/water-facts/water/